The Beat Generation and the Popular Novel
in the United States, 1945–1970

The Beat Generation and the Popular Novel in the United States, 1945–1970

by
THOMAS NEWHOUSE

McFarland & Company, Inc., Publishers
Jefferson, North Carolina, and London

Library of Congress Cataloguing-in-Publication Data

Newhouse, Thomas, 1950–
    The beat generation and the popular novel in the United
States, 1945–1970 / by Thomas Newhouse.
        p.   cm.
    Includes bibliographical references and index.
    ISBN 0-7864-0841-3 (softcover : 50# alkaline paper) ∞
    1. American fiction — 20th century — History and criticism.
    2. Popular literature — United States — History and criticism.
    3. Beat generation in literature.   4. Beat generation.   I. Title.
PS374.P63N49 2000
813'.5409 — dc21   00-24223

British Library Cataloguing-in-Publication data are available

Manufactured in the United States of America

McFarland & Company, Inc., Publishers
    Box 611, Jefferson, North Carolina 28640
        www.mcfarlandpub.com

Contents

Acknowledgments

I owe debts to all those who have read the manuscript. I am especially grateful to Marcus Klein for his valuable advice and acute criticisms throughout the early stages of this project. I would also like to thank Leslie Fiedler, who has been an immense source of encouragement as long as I have known him. And I am grateful to Mark Shechner for his keen editorial eye and for his numerous suggestions regarding the first version of the manuscript.

Special thanks go to David Karnath, with whom I discussed many of the finer points raised by the book's primary sources and whose insights on the ideological implications of the texts were most valuable to me. Finally, I am indebted to my wife, Sheila, and to my daughter, Amanda, for their patience and support during the writing of this book.

Introduction

The importance of the Beat Generation as a general influence on the counterculture of the 1960s has long been noted by cultural historians. The Beat agenda, a virtual catalogue of oppositional preferences, is legend: they championed all forms of sexual and spiritual liberation; they celebrated candor, risk, and individuality; and they opposed materialism, censorship, and the mass media. These were among the values and social codes also embraced by a disaffected youth culture coming to prominence a decade after the Beats exploded on the public consciousness in America.

The Beats' literary legacy, however, is more difficult to determine than their cultural one. It is commonplace nowadays to find sympathetic critics who point out the various misstatements and unfair judgments made by conservative critics, or who condemn the mass culture's often outrageous distortions of the Beat message and lifestyle in moronic exploitative parodies presented at the time of the initial Beat public exposure in the late 1950s. But while such revisionism is indeed a necessary and worthy enterprise, it has done little to shed light on the Beats' place in the literature of this century.

Critical studies of the Beats have frequently linked them to other bohemian movements that flourished at the same historical moment, many of which became better known as a result of their association with the Beat writers. As has been frequently pointed out, Beat writing was part of a general oppositional and experimental current in the arts of the 1950s that included the Black Mountain School, the New York poets, the writers of the San Francisco Renaissance, Abstract-Expressionist painters, and even experimental filmmakers like Robert Frank, Shirley Clarke, Stan Brakhage, and Kenneth Anger. Bringing these disparate artists together was a shared aesthetic that opposed objectivity and declared the uniqueness of reality by emphasizing the commonplace and displaying a preference for open forms and candid personal content.

In addition to having a similar literary aesthetic, the new writers disdained the intellectual establishment, aiming their contempt, in equal measure, at both the New Critics and the New York intellectuals. Both of those established literary camps had the academy as their base, and although it could be said that the New York intellectuals emphasized the political and social functions of literature as the New Critics did not, both agreed that formal excellence should remain the standard in literary art. The work of the young writers, personal and idiosyncratic, a discourse of resistance and experiment, was generally ignored or lambasted by the critical establishment, which had difficulty judging it by the usual standards of criticism. Thus, the young writers abjured the usual scholarly outlets such as *Kenyon Review, Hudson Review,* and *Sewanee Review* and, like modernist writers before them, sought to project their message through small presses and underground or desktop publications such as *Exodus, Big Table,* and *Evergreen Review,* often forming alliances with kindred spirits to promote their art. Beat affiliation with other artistic or literary movements was in essence an attempt by disillusioned artists to establish a unified front to assault the established social and artistic institutions of the time.

While all these generalizations are more or less matters of historical fact, the details concerning the associations provide a less tidy picture. Certainly the history of the period reveals more tension and discord — more social and artistic incompatibility among the new artists — than it does unity and consistent aims. Relationships that were formed between the Beats and other literary movements were usually generated through the tireless promotional efforts of Allen Ginsberg. It was Ginsberg's dynamic reading of *Howl* at the Six Gallery in 1955 that provided the inspiration for what turned out to be a brief period of harmony between the Beats and the San Francisco Renaissance, the literary group with which the Beats had the most intimate connection. But Jack Kerouac and Gregory Corso were often socially antagonistic to members of that group; some of the dominating literary figures of San Francisco looked on them as coarse interlopers attempting to exploit what was already an established movement and to dominate the spotlight. Though they did have an important impact on a few of the San Francisco writers — specifically, Michael McClure, Lawrence Ferlinghetti, and Philip Whalen — Beat writers were never fully integrated into the West Coast literary movement. Moreover, one of the major Beat figures, William Burroughs, the man who had mentored the intellectual attitudes of the Beats, was actually living abroad during that time, having no contact whatsoever with the San Francisco scene. As for the Black Mountain School, any comparison between the Beats and Black Mountain mentor Charles Olson may easily dim the parallels. According to Martin Duberman, Olson was "a decidedly cerebral man. He valued learning and the cognitive process far more than, say, a Corso or Kerouac, and his orientation remained far more rooted in Western culture than, say, Ginsberg's."[1]

What seemed to set the Beats — Ginsberg, Burroughs, and Kerouac — apart from their peers was a deep, disturbing alienation that transcended their identities as artists and extended to personal idiosyncrasy and a self-destructive bent. Such tendencies were captured in an intellectual fascination, perhaps even an identification, with outcasts and criminals. To be sure, their project was in large part an attempt to reveal, in the most intimate detail, the world of the outcast.

To the Beats, America had become a spiritual wasteland, a land of intolerable repression and conformity, and extreme measures were needed to overcome the restrictions placed on the individual. Of course, the Beats were not alone in attacking the shortcomings of the masses. Nonliterary figures like Wilhelm Reich, especially in *Listen, Little Man* (1948); David Reisman, in *The Lonely Crowd* (1950); C. Wright Mills, in *White Collar* (1951) and *The Power Elite* (1956) had paved the way for the new consciousness by expressing contempt for the passive, well-adjusted consumer. But with the exception of Reich, an important influence on early Beat writing, the Beats offered the most radical solutions to social anonymity. Agreeing with the sociologists that true individuality was not to be found in the high-rises of corporate America or in the ordered existence of middle-class suburbia, the Beats sought liberation through hedonistic self-indulgence and found companionship and spiritual kinship with those on the margins of society — addicts, thieves, and dropouts. Ginsberg's *Howl* and the novels of Burroughs and Kerouac all chronicled the lives of marginal individuals — some of them dangerous, amoral psychopaths who lived impulsively and attacked every notion of normality embraced by the bland guardians of middle-class existence. While this aspect of their work does not by itself explain the whole appeal and importance of Beat authors, it does much to explain the resonance of the Beat image in the popular culture of their own time as well as their continued visibility in the cultural marketplace.

Introduction

Such intimate identification with the outcasts of society was not something other bohemian artists with whom the Beats have often been connected necessarily cared to endorse. Nor could it be said that indulgence in sex and drugs as part of a liberation program was condoned by all Beat associates. Among the artistic groups with which they briefly connected, the Beats were unique in establishing the importance of a radical lifestyle as one element in the liberation of the individual spirit. Yet if an endorsement of outlawry was not forthcoming from San Francisco poets or New York artists, meditations on such patterns of behavior through the postwar period may be detected in other places, not exclusively but most frequently in the novel, and often in narratives that have not been placed within the context of the Beat project.

In this study I attempt to show that the impulse for liberation existed in the wider cultural experience of the time and was represented in a variety of narratives, not just in the handful of Beat works available to us. I have chosen to call this body of work the underground narrative, unified by its candid treatment of taboo subjects and its generally oppositional purpose. Many of the underground narratives I will explore are the work of writers who chronicled the lives of social types and who sought to establish an alternative mode of community that many felt had been destroyed by the Second World War. These narratives reflect their attempts to recover a loss of potential or to channel their energies into alternative social forms and to abandon constraints in order to embrace new experience. This activity is depicted in both older and newer trends in American fiction within the period 1945–1970, from social protest city fiction of the immediate postwar time, which drew on social realism (juvenile delinquent potboilers), to urban nightmare (narratives about hipsters, drug addicts, and the early Beats) and looser experimental narratives (later Beats, Burroughs, Alexander Trocchi, Robert Stone) to consciously politicized versions of the underground view (Mailer, homoerotic fiction, some New Journalism).

This study, then, is not merely an attempt to expand the Beat canon, though the Beat Generation certainly played a central role in the formulation of the literary consciousness that has surrounded the underground mystique and will be prominently considered. More specifically, this is a study of the literary response in fiction to the spiritual malaise that grew from dark cold war realities affecting artists and intellectuals immediately after the Second World War, a response that reached its fullest expression in the counterculture of the 1960s.

4

Introduction

While there is much overlap of activity in the underground narrative — for example, Beat novels often feature drug use and homosexuality — certain distinctions can be made both by emphasis and by definition. I have organized the books for discussion according to genre; thus it has been necessary to select fiction from a variety of writers whose narratives are linked by subject matter only. That is, Nelson Algren will be considered alongside William Burroughs because both writers chose drug addiction as subject, not because they emerged from the same traditions or even shared the same views of the drug subculture. Indeed, Burroughs and John Rechy are more "underground" — more formally experimental and radical in their visions — than, say, Gore Vidal or James Baldwin, though all of these writers wrote important novels about the homosexual subculture. And most writers who wrote about juvenile delinquency were actually liberals or former leftists committed to a rationalist or sociologist approach to the material. Moreover, their methods and values were often contrary to those practiced by writers who aligned themselves with the underground and who believed that stylistic innovation and social disaffiliation were necessary and perhaps even inevitable responses to cultural malaise after the war. At the same time, these disparate voices testified to the emergence of a cultural phenomenon that gained strength throughout the 1950s and 1960s. Whether or not the authors were opposed to commercial sensibility (most underground narratives can be defined by their lower-depth and real-life subject matter more than by the experimentalist mission to privilege method over content), the books they wrote made a previously hidden world visible, providing an inside track to the secret world of drugs, forbidden sex, and the arcane rituals of a personal and social underworld. Something was happening, and it was the American writer who stepped forward to acknowledge and chronicle it.

While the Beat Generation and its avant-garde colleagues of the new consciousness are often credited with providing important contexts for subsequent countercultural developments such as gay liberation and the drug culture before those movements attracted widespread attention, full endorsement of the utopian spirit is conspicuously absent from the underground narrative. Idealism is frequently subverted by self-vitiating tendencies toward aggressiveness, by moral distancing, destructive impulses, and insufficiently formulated social codes. Because most writers of underground novels were primarily interested in capturing the process of history as it passed from possibility into actuality, they discarded the romance

5

inherent in the alternatives that were seemingly being proposed. Instead, the underground writer dramatized the dark moral paradox that has not only characterized the Beat project but has defined the American experience itself.

Yet as writers came to explore those special qualities in the hipster, the nonconformist street punk, and the rebel outcast, or presented new subject matter, or sought to express themselves in ways inconsistent with or oppositional to their society, the new man gathered substance, achieving uniqueness and cultural identity. In the postwar period the struggle between marginal and mainstream took on unprecedented importance, and with it began a unique period in literary and cultural history that challenged the humanistic grounds on which American literature is based.

Hail the ambiguous fathers, and look closely at
them, they are the unadmitted, the club of Themselves
weary riders, but who sit upon the landscape as the
Great Stones. And only have fun among themselves.
They are the lonely ones

Hail them, and watch out. The rest of us, on the
beach as we had previously known it, did not know
there was this left side. As they came in riding from the
sea — we did not notice them until they were already
creating the beach we had not known was there — but
we assume they came in from the sea. We assume that.
We don't know.

—*Charles Olson*

Forerunners: The Underground Tradition

The publication of Kenneth Rexroth's essay "Disengagement: The Art of the Beat Generation" in *New World Writing* in 1957 was a major step toward legitimizing a generation of underground writers in America. Rexroth, an established poet and critic by the late 1950s, was no stranger to controversy; since the 1930s he had been involved with avant-garde literary movements and leftist political groups. Often at the center of such activities, here he was a peripheral figure, less active participant than fascinated observer and supportive commentator attempting to explain the relevance of the underground stance. Rexroth viewed the young literary rebels as kindred spirits engaged in an official battle with highbrow culture, their sights set on exposing blandness and corruption. "It is impossible for an artist to remain true to himself as a man let alone an artist, and work within the context of this society," Rexroth wrote.

Rexroth dismisses "the deliberately and painfully intellectual fiction which appears in the literary quarterlies" and celebrates the popular novel, which he calls "the only significant fiction in America."[1] Rexroth, a well-known poet, was usually somewhat condescending about fiction, a literary form more conducive than poetry to earning fame and fortune for authors. But his use of the generic term "popular novel" was intended to give distinction to a type of prose work whose most characteristic feature is apparently its honest and intriguing subject matter.

> Much of the best popular fiction deals with the world of the utterly disaffiliated. Burlesque and carnival people, hipsters, handicappers and hopheads, wanted men on the lam, an expendable squad of soldiers being expended, anyone who by definition has been divorced from society and cannot afford to

believe even an iota of the social lie — these are the favorite characters of modern fiction.[2]

Marginal figures had of course long inhabited the pages of the American novel. Cooper's noble savages, Twain's restless adolescents, Steinbeck's layabout paisanos, Farrell's tough young urbanites, London's crude wanderers all constitute social types with behavioral codes, social aims, and moral standards contrary to those of the dominant society. But Rexroth was observant in defining a literary phenomenon that was being formulated via the sudden influx of Beat writers. Indeed, Rexroth instinctively perceived that postwar American fiction represented a unique view of social and cultural bifurcation. In the absence of the radical politics that had informed much fiction about marginality before 1940 and had maintained victim status for most social outsiders, many American writers of the postwar period were celebrating the freedom of marginality, particularly in light of growing materialism, affluence, and technological progress. In their novels drug use, obsessive wandering, open sexuality, and even violence, all adversarial responses to mainstream social and political life, constituted a rejection of standard modes of behavior. The rebel outlaws of the postwar period actively resisted totalitarian demands of order. Insisting on radical notions of freedom, these postwar writers served as counteragents in conflict with a larger, blander culture. Underground writing seemed vital because it proposed a program of cultural anarchy working toward self-liberation, breakthrough, and new life.

Rexroth's labeling the new visionaries "popular writers" may have been a poet's grudging acknowledgment of the commercial potential of novelists. But in retrospect it also demonstrated his awareness of the ambivalent relationship that has always existed between the various condemned outsiders he mentions and the status quo. While most of the subgroups and social types mentioned in Rexroth's essay have been despised by a majority culture, there has nevertheless been a paradoxical curiosity on the part of members of the dominant society to understand and even an urge to admire the marginal experience for its freedom at the same time as they seek to neutralize outsiders as a threat to civilization. American fiction has reserved a special place for the outcast whose life is written and read about by those who least resemble him. In a time of apparent mass conformity, such literature had profound meaning and, consequently, great potential to create an impact on the public consciousness.

Genre fiction, then being mass-produced by the burgeoning paper-back industry, had long given evidence of the public's infatuation with sex, deviance, and the darker places of society. Lee Server has noted that

> from these paperback "originals" there began to emerge, along with the steady supply of Westerns and whodunits, distinctive new styles of commercial fiction full of gritty realism, frankly erotic, lacking in sentiment or conventional morality, and with an iconoclastic eagerness to explore the controversial and the taboo. Whole genres would develop around such shocking sub-ject matter as drug addiction, racism, homosexuality, and juve-nile delinquency.[3]

Hard-boiled classics emerged from the pens of such legendary pulp writers as Jim Thompson, David Goodis, Cornell Woolrich, Gil Brewer, Hal Ellson, and Charles Willeford, to name a few. Stylistically and com-mercially, the early works of Beat writers shared many features with the frank realism of the best writers in the crime genre. Both John Clellon Holmes's *Go* (1952) and William Burroughs's *Junkie* (1953), each depict-ing the low-life activities of various urban types, first appeared as Ace paperback originals. Burroughs's book was published as part of an Ace double with *Narcotic Agent*, a novel whose cover boasted that its contents dramatized the "Gripping True Adventures of a T-Man's War Against the Dope Menace." Moreover, Dashiell Hammett had been an early model for Beat writers to study as they searched for a literary style to express the new vision. Dennis McNally has noted that "Hammett's world was like theirs, a piece of black and white and gray, anything but 'clean, orderly, and sane.'"[4] Appropriately, William Burroughs and Jack Kerouac collaborated in the 1940s on an unpublished, Hammettesque crime novel titled *And the Hippos Were Boiled in Their Tanks*, a book that recalled the atmosphere and events that had taken place in Greenwich Village while Kerouac was a student at Columbia University, its central focus being Lucien Carr's murder of David Kammerer. Kerouac would return to a writer he admired in his youth, Thomas Wolfe, to inspire his first novel, *The Town and the City* (1950), but Burroughs remained indebted to Hammett's hard-boiled prose style and bleak vision of society throughout his career.

Despite having among its ranks creators of real talent, crime fiction offered by the softcover industry varied widely in quality. This was also the case with underground fiction, for when the Beats achieved a level of notoriety with the publication of Kerouac's *On the Road*, many would-be popular authors jumped on the bandwagon. Numerous Beat exploitation novels were published in the late fifties, flashing such titles as *Epitaph for a Dead Beat*, *Beatnik Wanton*, and *Bang a Beatnik*. But the type of novel endorsed by Rexroth was not without literary merit. Though few names are mentioned in his essay, Rexroth does refer to Jack Kerouac and Nelson Algren as definitive practitioners of popular literature that "coming up, meets high-brow literature coming down."[5] That is, these authors were writing a kind of fiction in which the vulgar and the sublime meet, their books occupying a place in which the popular novel and the work of high art intersect. This synthesis of high art and genre fiction may also be attributed to some of the European writers Rexroth identifies as highbrow novelists whom he believed had a substantial influence on American underground writers, the most prominent being Louis Ferdinand Celine and Jean Genet.

The dark pessimism of Celine, especially in *Journey to the End of the Night* (1932) and *Death on the Installment Plan* (1934), did indeed have a profound impact on the Beats when they were formulating their literary project. Both of these books, along with Oswald Spengler's *The Decline of the West*, were read by the small circle of Beat authors and made a direct impact on the new vision. The immersion of Celine's protagonists in an insane, catastrophic war-torn Europe reflected their own experience as young explorers of social and psychic reality encountering irrational forces in the postwar America in which they lived. Moreover, Celine's innovative voice, his emphasis on argot and his ability to capture the hallucinatory quality of the experiences of his narrators, also attracted writers who sought to express themselves through modified realistic literary forms. It was of central importance that Celine's deeply subversive point of view prevented his being identified with a humanist tradition.

Though Genet was not an innovator in his use of language, he, even more than Celine, captured the dualistic essence of the best underground writing. Profoundly contemptuous of bourgeois values, Genet not only sympathized with the outcast underclass heroes of his fiction, but he elevated them to the level of aristocracy. This glamorous vision of the outcast as hero, derived from Genet's own experience as a Parisian wanderer and thief, accorded with popular models familiar to Genet from his extensive reading. According to Edmund White, Genet's "way of perceiving men and boys around him was colored by the tinted lenses of high and low literature."[6] At the agricultural penitentiary colony in Mettray where he spent his adolescence, Genet devoured the books of Paul Feval, Xavier de Montepin, Ponson du Terrail, Pierre Decourcelle, and especially Emile Gaboriau, "the father of the crime novel in France."[7] Later Genet befriended Francis Carco, who specialized in fiction of Paris lowlife and who was an important literary influence on the young writer. Carco was a pioneer of the type of fiction Rexroth discusses, and long before Genet, he established "racy dialogue in thiefs' and whores' dialect; poetic passages of narration and description in a highly sophisticated, educated French; and a sociological but sympathetic fascination with low-life folkways."[8]

Genet was also familiar with the works of Rimbaud, Baudelaire, and Dostoyevsky, central literary influences on Beat writers, and he took pains to incorporate elements of their work into his own. The highbrow element was Genet's employment of elegant, classic literary French, the language of the oppressor, which he took to stunning poetic levels in describing the most debased activities of his characters. Unlike Celine, who created an intriguing mixture of argot and classic French, Genet felt that "he had to address the torturer precisely in his own language."[9]

The Beats and other underground writers who came after them were also great synthesizers of esoteric and popular forms. Aspiring to be both avant-garde and popular at the same time, the Beats drew on pop culture materials like jazz, radio, comics, movies, and of course hard-boiled crime fiction for the substance of their myths. Simultaneously, they were self-avowed experimentalists who were sympathetic to the idea of an avant-garde. They professed to have a kindred spirit with method actors, modern dancers, abstract expressionist painters, and free-form poets, all of whom, like the early modernists, were launching assaults on tradition by being formally innovative. But the Beat writers did not share the view of many modernist experimenters who were fleeing from the vulgarities of the modern wasteland that innovative formal approaches to art were necessary to revive a flagging cultural heritage. The Beats were less interested in creating a lasting and coherently expressed art object or in purifying essential form than they were in generating a heightened participation in reality, not a reflection of the real.

Jack Kerouac was the exemplary devaluator of the art object. Insisting that it is the act of creation — the creation of the experience of life itself — and not the completed art work that gives vitality and meaning to the artist's efforts, Kerouac created a string of narratives designed to bring the immediacy of the experience to the page. Some critics were baffled by Kerouac's aesthetic excesses, struggling in vain to find meaning both in the many road adventures of *On the Road* and in his spontaneous prose style. They demanded that more substantial solutions to the problems of identity be proposed in a novel or that a protagonist in a novel seek to find his place in the scheme of the society in which he lives. One reviewer of Kerouac's novel asserted that the book "is not a significant social document: the people in it represent too negligible a portion of the millions of Americans who mold our culture."[10] *On the Road*, however, testified to being nothing more than one man's engagement and struggle with experience. If the novel was nontraditional and antiformalist, it was this way simply because life was more important than art, and "ordinary" subjects and traditional forms were not adequate to express the changing face of America at mid-century.

Beat writing was thus a project to make reality directly known. The myth of the superiority of immediate experience over that of derivative experience was central to the Beat myth. It is this quality that separated the American underground from its European counterparts like Celine and Genet, though both of these writers were engaged, like the underground writers in America, in breaking down the barriers between life and art. But the Beats and the writers they inspired attempted to capture a fuller range of experience than did Celine, who was relentless in his pessimism. And no one would mistake Genet's elegant posturing as anything but a carefully crafted assault on his presumably bourgeois readers.

Notwithstanding its European influences, the Beat movement was quintessentially American. Kerouac's books especially held sacred the tradition of the liberated self as celebrated in the writings of Emerson, Thoreau, and particularly Whitman, who combined cosmic vision with a vulgar and sensuous reality. Whitman's message, written nearly a century before urban bohemians sought radical departure from conventionality, materialism, and conformity, announced something of a credo for postwar disaffiliates hungering for meaning and floundering in what they regarded as a dead civilization. The Beats' Whitmanesque insistence on taking to nature, on indulging in the outrageous and irrational, on demonstrating the true self, and on being skeptical of tradition was meaningful to the writers of the underground who faced the bland realities of the moment. Moreover, Whitman embodied the literary traditions, essentially populist ones, that sustained the Beat movement: American Bohemia and the hobo myth.

Bohemianism, of course, originated in France during the time of Balzac, but, as Clement Greenberg wrote in 1948, "The alienation of Bohemia was only an anticipation in nineteenth Century Paris; it is in New York that it has completely been fulfilled."[11] In their early stages these traditions had radical-utopian agendas, but by the time they impacted the underground, both had undergone significant alterations.

Bohemians of the postwar underground, whether from Venice Beach or Greenwich Village, were a different breed from the youthful dissenters of the 1910s and 1920s. Though some of the practices were the same — free love, devotion to art, and endless chatter about both in cafes and bars — there had been a prominent political component in the early bohemian circles of Greenwich Village inhabited by Floyd Dell, Mabel Dodge, and Max Eastman. Indeed, the old bohemians were as quick to rally to social causes such as the strike of the textile workers in Patterson, New Jersey, as they were to flock to the Armory Exhibition of International Art in 1913. The early-twentieth-century bohemian rebellion, though sparked by modernism, had continuity with nineteenth-century bohemian impulses. According to Martin Green, "artists felt the need to free their art from complicity with bourgeois taste and with its origins in the bourgeois state. Responding to the same historical facts as the socialists and in some ways in step with them, the painters rebelled against their society."[12]

But the bohemian who combined politics and art ultimately had difficulty maintaining intellectual independence as he sought a proletarian art to serve the revolutionary message. Eventually, most political radicals equated bohemia with bourgeois apathy. In a memo addressed to members of the John Reed Club, Joseph Freeman expressed an intolerance for bohemians who associated with the radical movement but who failed to fully embrace communism: "A bohemian is a person who has broken with his social class; hence he has no social roots; the old ideology is gone and no new ideology has taken its place." That is, a bohemian was simply one who failed to join the political struggle, since with active membership he would "cease to be a bohemian."[13]

The bohemians of the 1940s and 1950s, on the other hand, had no problems reconciling their subversive individualism with an allegiance to politics or with sustaining both a devotion to avant-garde culture and a political radicalism. If, as Leslie Fishbein has noted, "village radicals were constantly torn between imperatives and political beliefs,"[14] in postwar bohemia ideological dissent gave way to total obsession with self. It called for living life at the limits in order to come into contact with one's deepest impulses. It was a lifestyle characterized by pure anarchy, apparently untrammeled by politics of any kind.

But by the late 1950s, the Village had also become a genuine community of artists devoted to radicalizing the arts. According to Fred McDarrah, "Everybody knew everybody, and it was like a family get-together. Painting, poetry, music, dance, and off-Broadway theater were in full swing; abstract painters threw globs of paint on canvases; poets shouted Beat words at enthralled cafe crowds. Everybody was creating something."[15]

Gatherings at the Artist's Studio and at coffee houses on Bleecker and MacDougal, such as the Gaslight, Cafe Bizarre and Epitome, gave the Beats a forum to present their work. And places like the Cedar Street Tavern and the Five Spot, a jazz club frequently patronized by Beat writers, provided less formal opportunities for bohemian artists to discuss their projects.

The hobo mystique was as continuous a line as bohemianism, notwithstanding its having undergone its own transformations. The archetype for it may be found in narratives by writers such as Jim Tully and Jack London — tales of tough vagabonds with a hostility to the bourgeois values of work and family, who take to the road and cultivate a manly stoicism as hard-boiled and emotionally controlled as any Hemingway hero. The image was modified in the thirties in social protest literature, which, as Kingsley Widmer points out, gave "a considerable place to the wandering consciousness, though it may also attenuate the tough vitality and sense of freedom for purposes of didactic pathos."[16] Though individualism was not eviscerated in such fiction, leftist writers of the thirties nonetheless perceived marginal figures as victims of a cruel society. The social protest fiction of Dos Passos and Steinbeck primarily fostered the image of the alienated wanderer defeated by his social circumstances. In Whitman the road had led to joy, diversity of experience, and divine self-revelation; for Tully, London, and Vachel Lindsay the road had led to heightened individuality and crucial self-awareness; but for the Okie or the dispossessed hobo the road led only to suffering and victimization. Proletarian fiction demonstrated that the road no longer symbolized America's promise of opportunity. Widmer argues that the victimized wanderer of such fiction, as opposed to the hobo explorer of the original archetype,

> serves to confirm American freedom — the openness of the road — but then reveals that it is really compulsive and destructive, thus re-enforcing our refusal of freedom. This mythos of the hoboing experience, which variously appears in a far wider range of fiction than so-called naturalism, often oddly uses the man down-and-out in apologetics for the way in-and-up.[17]

If Widmer's analysis is accurate, and I believe it is, it follows that it was necessary to avoid confirming or reinforcing success myths that were central to the corrupt mainstream social order that a literature of dissent, political or otherwise, was attacking. The road could remain a valid metaphor for freedom only if it led away from social entrapment to a new kind of fulfillment — in essence, by reverting to the flavor of the original archetype. It is no wonder that, though many leftist writers and critics had an aesthetic bias for the naturalistic wanderer of the thirties, they had difficulty embracing his descendant in the new version presented by Kerouac and others.

Ironically, it was in this atmosphere of politically charged dissent that the underground tradition begun in Whitman continued. Without affirming political solutions, the writers who would influence the underground narrative in the postwar era wanted to present experience that was contrary to the programmatic thinkers and protesters who used literature as a tool for social change. One alternative path was to internalize the rebellion, to derive meaning from the reality that one perceives, and to break free of cultural conditioning by allowing discovery to transform the self — to savor the energy that all experience, even the most calamitous, has on the growth of the spirit.

Thomas Wolfe made the opening move in this direction. A writer of enormous energy, Wolfe wrote fiction that was impressionistic, formless, intense, and, most important, subjective. Wolfe's personalization of the materials of his fiction, transforming experience into artistic vision, was a general influence on many postwar writers, especially Jack Kerouac, Norman Mailer, James Jones, and John Rechy, in whose work a fragile sense of reality shifts ground as remembered events are sifted through the artist's consciousness. Wolfe's prose reinstates the importance of spiritual forces on the evolving self and usually details the exploits of a questing young

The Web and the Rock, Dell edition, 1960.

man, sensitive to everything, whose self-exposure leads to wisdom and human connection.

This apolitical personalization of experience, a liberation in the voice, was continued in Henry Miller who, even more than Wolfe, made a dramatic impact on postwar underground writing. Miller's contribution was to use this new disorderly literary self-dramatization as a way to transcend the problems that politically ánd socially minded writers of the thirties had faced. Such writers made marginal outcasts unwise and self-defeated victims of a struggle to locate avenues of freedom. Miller, a romantic anarchist and antihumanist, saw no solution to the turbulent decade in the utopia of a radical agenda. Jay Martin wrote, "He couldn't believe in reform or political change; when all civilization was defective, one simply chose the system that best suited him with no utopian illusions. His rebelliousness worried the Conservatives, while his detachment disturbed his radical acquaintances."[18]

With his characteristic political indifference, Miller's response to the chaos he saw everywhere around him was to celebrate it. "Chaos is the score upon which reality is written," declares Miller in the opening pages of *Tropic of Cancer* (1934).

> Everywhere I go people are making a mess of their lives. Everyone has his private tragedy. It's in the blood now — misfortune, grief, and suicide. The atmosphere is saturated with disaster, frustration, futility.... However, the effect upon me is exhilarating. Instead of being discouraged or depressed, I enjoy it. I am crying for more and more disasters, for bigger calamities, for grander failures, I want the whole world to be out of whack.[19]

Miller's perverse rage proceeded from what he saw as the failure of a diseased society and a burned-out culture, as well as a personal failure as husband, writer, and citizen, which gave him total freedom to pursue an agenda of outraged vengeance. Failure was the precondition for Miller's attacks on America and for the activities engaged by the bitter expatriate-drifting, writing, starving, committed only to survival, expecting nothing and yet strangely content. Miller was thus compelled to seek out life, the absurdity and incongruity of which gave him occasions for great joy.

But not only did hitting rock bottom allow Miller to be happily free of American delusion; it allowed him to see with clarity that which had previously been hidden — that from which commitment to mainstream values had cut him off. This urge to see was transformed into confession, of course, but also into purifying vision, a surreal catalogue of revelation — sights and sounds depicting the nature of the contemporary apocalypse.

> ...wandering, and going mad with the beauty of it, ... the women sleeping on newspapers, sleeping in the rain; everywhere the musty porches of the cathedrals and beggars and lice and old hags full of St. Vitus dance; pushcarts stacked up like barrels in the side streets, the smell of berries in the marketplace and the old church surrounded with vegetables and blue arc lights, the gutter slippery with garbage and women in satin pumps staggering through the filth and vermin at the end of an all-night souse.[20]

In his urge to absorb all experience, Miller sought to record "all that which is omitted from books"[21] and to call into question all preconceived attitudes held by his readership.

With no allegiance to the middle-class world, Miller was given flexibility to defy the morality of bourgeois existence. Apart from his apocalyptic statements, the narrative concerns Miller's marginal life and the lives of his eccentric friends — Boris, Van Norden, Fillmore, and Carl — all hustlers, spongers, and sexual thrill seekers. Not only do the nasty misadventurers of these men betray a grand and merry moral corruption, but they reflect Miller's stated intention to create the new individual, certainly no stranger to fiction — the outlaw from middle-class respectability sharing a spiritual kinship with the author. Miller's legacy may be seen in the exuberant outcasts of Kerouac and in all fictional postwar disaffiliates who provided a sense of authenticity apart from adherence to expected, bourgeois patterns of behavior. These are men who, by matters of circumstances and sensibility, seek ecstasy in the moment — less existential wanderers than urban adventurers, galvanized into action by an absence of meaningful social engagement or by vengeance against a hypocritical society. Miller's rallying cry sounded the credo of the postwar outcast. "I've lived out my melancholy youth. I don't give a fuck anymore what's behind me. I'm Healthy. Incurably healthy. No sorrow, no regrets. No past, no future. The present is enough for me. Today! Le bel aujourd'hui!"[22]

Like Wolfe, Miller celebrated the special qualities of the artist, though Miller was different from Wolfe inasmuch as he was himself both artist and underdog outcast. But it became clear that Miller's artist-saint was inclusive in the modernist project of redeeming the wounded spirit in a vulgar flawed world as much as he was a vehicle by which to protest and attack hypocrisy in the manner of D. H. Lawrence. This became especially evident upon Miller's return to America, where his particular form of literary rebellion quickly became mannered.

In *The Air-Conditioned Nightmare* (1945), another variation of the bum-on-the-warpath book that Miller had presented so effectively in the *Tropic* books and that given a more open and sensitive orientation, could have been an interesting predecessor to Kerouac's road books, Miller seemed more capable of parodying himself than of seeing America fresh. Perhaps without the poverty and true degradation that had made the marginal man in the early books perceive so well, and that had transformed the marginal man into a visionary, Miller could only resort to enlarging the artist's persona and to sharpening his invective. After a while, Miller's diatribes on American materialism become predictable, his complaints about the plight of the artist tedious, and his gestures to being down-and-out meaningful more in terms of the car he rides in, which keeps breaking down, than to a tattered condition of the spirit. The Miller voice is all there is, and too often the reader finds little connection between Miller's attacks on an America that denies its artists their just rewards and the travelogue he narrates.

Yet Miller's first-person narratives were major influences on the postwar American underground narrative, the personal voice best conveying disgust and dismay over a rotten and fragmented society. And there were other notable forerunners. Kenneth Patchen, a visionary poet in the tradition of Blake and Whitman, acknowledged, as did Miller, the imminent cultural apocalypse at the same time as he asserted life-affirming values to counter it. Open to the world, confronting life in all of its ugliness, Patchen provided an important model for the Beats and other underground writers. Patchen's iconoclastic spirit is best reflected in two remarkable prose works, *The Journal of Albion Moonlight* (1941) and *Sleepers Awake* (1945). Both books formulate a statement on behalf of Patchen's own pacifistic resistance to World War II and were formally indebted to surrealistic predecessors like Lautreamont's *Les Chants du Maldoror* and Rimbaud's *A Season in Hell* in their use of fantasy and structural fragmentation, nightmare imagery, and bitter ribaldry. Patchen also indulged in interests made familiar from his poetry, including his numerous drawings, typographical explosions, and use of pop culture, especially parodies of pulp

The Air-Conditioned Nightmare, Panther edition, 1965.

science fiction and hard-boiled detective fiction anticipating Burroughs. Patchen was also, along with Kenneth Rexroth and Langston Hughes, a pioneer in the jazz/poetry movement, often reading his poems to musical accompaniment at San Francisco's Blackhawk jazz club and on college campuses. Patchen's jazz play, *Don't Look Now*, was performed off-Broadway, and he made two recordings with the Chamber Jazz Sextet. Patchen's attempts to capture the emotional attitudes of jazz were profoundly influential on Beat writers of the fifties.

Another writer who was influential on the underground ethos, though to a lesser degree than Wolfe, Miller, or Patchen, was Paul Bowles. For the postwar underground writer who perceived the world as dark and threatening and attacked the smug limitations of bourgeois civilization, the early novels of Bowles, *The Sheltering Sky* (1949) and *Let It Come Down* (1952), and the early short stories, especially "The Delicate Prey" and "Pages from Cold Point," struck a chord. Bowles's novels and stories usually dramatize disastrous forays by middle-class characters fleeing bourgeois order into remote regions. These desperate flights to strange locations, to the orgasm, and to the drug experience signaled the directions taken by many underground writers in the fifties and sixties. Bowles's second novel, *Let It Come Down*, ends with a Gidean acte gratuit, just the sort of violence that tantalized underground writers and provided a rationale for those who sought to free themselves from the tyranny of bourgeois morality. Bowles later wrote stories celebrating the psychically liberating qualities of kif (like marijuana, a derivative of the hemp plant), and in Tangiers, during the sixties, he formed a friendship with William Burroughs, who had read Bowles's books and had certainly been influenced by him. Norman Mailer once asserted that Bowles "opened up the world of Hip. He let in the murder, the drugs, the incest, the death of the Square ... the call of the orgy, the end of civilization."[23]

Despite the enormous influence of these authors on Beat writing, it is clear that each in his fashion initiated a project to elevate the special qualities of the artist. All had been part of the modernist attempt to privilege the artist's unique gifts, which alone offered redemption in a flawed world, and to celebrate the artist as the new man. Wolfe's novels, though uncontrolled and voluminous, were in many respects Joycean chronicles of the spiritual growth of the youthful and sensitive artist. Likewise, Miller's artist saint, though more rebellious than Wolfe's young artist, was also a tortured spirit besieged by philistines, proselytizing endlessly on the glory of art and its creators. Kenneth Patchen was the closest thing to an underground writer before the Beats, but Patchen eschewed the spirit of populism espoused by later underground writers. Patchen's work was designed to be influential on a small community of creative artists who made Patchen more cult hero than celebrity. Henry Miller once remarked that Patchen's "awesome silence"[24] suggested a refusal to compromise at any cost. And Paul Bowles's early novels captured the attention of the critics and the reading public alike, ostensibly because of his style — the cold and brilliant surfaces of his fiction. Bowles, unlike Wolfe, Miller, and Patchen, was absent from his work, a quality that led his biographer, Christopher Sawyer-Laucanno, to dub Bowles "the invisible spectator."[25] In fact, despite Bowles's ominous and prophetic subject matter, he was actually consistent with the New Critical tendencies of many other writers of the forties, notably the southern Gothicists, to create a fiction of surface. As Chester Eisinger has noted, in the fiction of writers like Bowles, Flannery O'Connor, and Truman Capote, "technique is all, or virtually all; the craft of fiction is always in the forefront of the writer's consciousness.... It conveys its meanings often by symbols, occasionally through the use of myths."[26]

Underground writers, on the other hand, preferred to inspire an audience, rather than to celebrate the solitary artist and the exalted function of literary art, or to create brilliant, highly structured discourses about the end of civilization.

The project of the Beats, which provided inspiration for other writers who focused on subcultures and outcasts, including the New Journalists, was to show a privileged view of the rapidly changing culture. The rebellious generation of the '40s, '50s, and '60s, addressing itself to a relatively narrow spectrum of the total population, set out to limit the kind of artistic self-projection of Wolfe, Miller, and Patchen. The narrator who identified with the hero of the action but who was himself not at the center of activity was a frequent device used by underground writers. In such a narrative, the artist could be inspired by and interpret the impact of the new for change in his own life (the narrator was often passive or ordinary enough to represent a typical young American) and on a larger culture. The narrator who is primarily an observer can be seen in John Clellon Holmes's *Go*, Chandler Brossard's *Who Walk in Darkness*, Kerouac's *On the Road*, Norman Mailer's *Barbary Shore*, and Ken Kesey's *One Flew Over the Cuckoo's Nest*.

Some popular fictions that are not quintessentially Beat, while not necessarily borrowing the technique, also detail the impact of an unconventional character on a middle-class hero. James Jones's *Some Came Running* (1957) and James Leo Herlihy's *All Fall Down* (1960) are two novels from the period that dramatize the problems of a character whose energies spin off in several directions at once. The new man in these novels was not the artist but rather the nonartist, the individual marginal man, the "psychopath" who lived on the edge, naturally, intuitively, according to his wits and instincts. Ken Kesey is a fascinating figure inasmuch as he embodies both artist-intellectual and individualist-adventurer, and his career represents a steady progression to emphasize the latter.

Beat writing suggested that in a world characterized by control systems, individuals can still matter — individuals who are felt presences, looming more overtly in the balance than statements made in the promotion of ideology or art. The celebration of the outcast and the open response to experience made by a character capable of change were in the postwar period subtle weapons against a conformist bourgeois society. Moreover, it was not necessary to enlist the aid of radical politics, as a thirties context had demanded. Whether turning outward to the road or inward to personal discovery, the underground writer insisted only on great intimacy with all that he encountered and a purity of perception.

The source of underground energy that pervaded the popular culture in the late 1950s and that had inspired the early Beat works was the hipster milieu. The hipster expressed indifference to mainstream values by immersing himself in an alternative lifestyle. An important element of hipsterism was the worship of bebop, the revolutionary jazz of the forties invented by Charlie Parker, Dizzy Gillespie, and Thelonious Monk. The hipster par excellence was the jazz musician himself. Bop not only seemed to emblematize the conflict of values between an older generation that loathed it and a younger one that embraced it, but it acutely expressed the mood of the time. John Litweiler has pointed out that "the music itself, with its broken phrasing, dislocated rhythms, frightening ecstasies, fractured ballads, and harrowing rhythms," perfectly captured the emotional condition of the marginal milieu. "Bop was not simply the product of a new sensibility; it expressed a new, more neurotic kind of nervous system."[27] Moreover, frenzied, on-the-spot improvising represented for the Beats freedom from rationality, a primitive abandonment of self-conscious discipline reflected not only in the forms their writing took but in the particulars of a shared perception. Because the music established the virtues of furious motion and intuition, it required a special way of listening. "You had to dig to know; your consciousness had to be at a certain level of evolution; you had to be able to intuit on the bias, to hear music being music, to comprehend the difference between the confining intelligence and the soul recording its own drift,"[28] explained John Clellon Holmes. Though rock eventually replaced jazz as the soundtrack of the underground, the place of rhythmic music as a form of release, a source of Dionysian ecstasy, remained a staple of underground culture.

But if the Beats wanted to live outside of society and to explore the profundities of the self, by no means did they reject a desire for community. What became apparent in all the early Beat writings was the belief that an alternative community of like-minded souls who felt as alienated from mainstream society as they did — and not one inhabited by artists alone — actually existed. Thus Kerouac's term "Beat Generation," Ginsberg's notion that a massive national nervous breakdown was underway, and John Clellon Holmes's celebration of a cult of youth — "the wild kids — all the junkies, musicians, collegian sailors, con men, teenage Raskolnikovs, parking-lot hipsters and their rootless, willing girls"[29] — indicated the existence of a new Gestalt, its adherents searching for release through tribal community rather than participation in a depersonalized society.

It should be noted here that other writers of the postwar period explored the individual self, but without the sense of cultural and social collusion that inspired the Beat writers, they arrived at significantly different conclusions. Joseph, the protagonist of Saul Bellow's first novel, *Dangling Man* (1944), cannot resolve the tensions between his responsibility to a subversive individualism and to his role in a society to which he feels he must belong but cannot accept. Joseph is drafted into the army and eventually rejects the freedom of self-determination he has sought throughout the novel. "Long live regimentation,"[30] cries Joseph as he is about to be inducted at the end of the novel, acknowledging his failure to achieve an autonomous self. For Bellow, exploration of the self led nowhere.

Bellow's novel underscores the struggle experienced by many writers with leftist backgrounds to come to terms with cold war ambiguity, conflicts that the younger writers were unaffected by. No longer able to advocate political radicalism as an ideal, the older writers foundered. Though in the forties, after the failure of the Old Left, intellectuals like Lionel Trilling tried to reform a flagging notion of liberalism — to reconfigure it to meet a complex moral reality — the struggle to link the individual to larger social processes came hard. "The old connection between literature and politics has been dissolved,"[31] wrote Trilling. Indeed, since there seemed to be no profit in recording the social madness through interior journeys into the self, leftists and liberals seemed to be at a standstill. Thus it was common for many former radicals to see the Beats' particular brand of revolt as self-indulgent and politically irresponsible escapism. As Thomas Hill Schaub has written, "Few were willing to acknowledge any substantial critique in the cultural politics of the new writing. This was especially the case with the Old Left: they claimed a continued commitment to radical politics on the one hand, while denying either the political or literary importance of the new generation on the other."[32] The new writers' obsession with immediacy and alternative culture and lifestyle — the hip consciousness as a way to locate truth — remained inaccessible or unacceptable to members of the cultural elite who had become reluctant standard bearers of an orthodox culture.

But despite the underground's apparent rejection of specifically political solutions, the desire for community would lend itself to a politicization of the marginal experience. The sympathies in underground writing derived from oppositional activities and expressed through modified realistic literary forms were eventually politicized, creating the spirit of the New Left in the 1960s, the politics of experience and experimental living displacing the Old Left's politics of Marx. As Christopher Lasch has pointed out, "Orthodox Marxism has had very little appeal for the young radicals of the sixties, partly because in their view it is plodding and unheroic, partly because they associate it with bureaucratic structures — whether embodied in political parties, corporations, or universities — which in turn are the principal objects of their anger."[33]

The nonconformist-existential ethos of the Beats ultimately became a political stance, but without roots in an ideological base, by the 1960s political resistance was manifested for the most part in acts of pure desperation. Lasch has asserted that "the search for personal integrity could lead only to a politics in which 'authenticity' was equated with the degree of one's alienation, the degree of one's willingness to undertake existential acts of definance."[34] In their opposition to rational choice as a viable mode for liberation, Beat writers, while not being overtly political, at least in terms that could be understood by members of the Old Left, set the tone for the radical revolt that would characterize the confrontational strategies of the New Left in the sixties. At the same time, the underground narrative, with its reliance on various modes of self-defeat that nullify its own program of salvation, also presaged the failure of leftist groups that would forge ahead in a similarly highly charged atmosphere of violence and social instability.

None of this of course was being foretold by sympathetic critics like Kenneth Rexroth. It was the young writers' creative energy and their apparent defiance of the cultural elite of New York intellectuals and New Critics that led Rexroth to announce his sympathies for the new underground writers in his essay, not their political potential. For Rexroth admits to a certain remoteness from the values inherent to underground narratives that seemed alien to his own social and intellectual orientation: "Social disengagement, artistic integrity, voluntary poverty — these are powerful virtues and may pull them through, but they are not the virtues we tried to inculcate — rather they are the exact opposite."[35] Not even an old anarchist like Rexroth was convinced that a revolt conceived in such exclusively cultural terms had much hope of succeeding.

It is important to emphasize that underground writers sought a revolution of the soul and a cultural revival, not a political revolution. Nevertheless, the new man, as conceived by postwar writers in all of the genres I will discuss, traveling from individual rebellion to an irrational confrontation with conspiratorial forces, would evolve from an ambiguous, threatening presence to a powerful force, undergoing vast transformations as America itself underwent change.

2

The War at Home:
The Novel of
Juvenile Delinquency

The notion that the new man was also an underground man, one who was liberated through action and suspension of rationality, was given expression persistently throughout the postwar era in the combat novel. Norman Mailer was the first war novelist to declare the death of liberalism in *The Naked and the Dead* (1948). In the collaboration between fascist ideologue General Cummings and vicious opportunist Sergeant Croft to destroy the liberal Hearn, disillusioned leftist Mailer created an appropriate metaphor to predict that the new man would find it necessary to bring the weapons of courage and instinct rather than his rationalized sympathies to bear in the war with the totalitarian oppressor on the home front.

Other writers of combat novels were not so willing to engage Mailer's combat metaphors for a domestic postwar America but nevertheless gave evidence of the vulnerable Everyman transformed into power-wielding warrior quickened by combat and merging with a purifying primitive life. Novels such as Harry Brown's *A Walk in the Sun* (1944) and James Jones's *The Thin Red Line* (1962) celebrated the vitality of average Americans who transformed their personal and cultural identities by engaging rules of violence and who achieved self-discovery in the process.

But the violence engaged in by troops in the Pacific and in Europe during the war had its analogue in American cities. As juvenile crime became a conspicuous fact during the war years and gang warfare emerged as a new phenomenon, sociologists and aspiring best-selling authors ventured forth to examine the problem. American authors in the immediate

postwar period, however, were not prepared to celebrate cultural muta-
tion in the new, the strange, and the disruptive that had emerged in the
dubious subcultural condition of America's youth embroiled in mutual and
generational conflict. Authors in fact tended toward conservative treatments of the subject, few acknowledging that urban delinquency signaled
the beginnings of a much larger cultural upheaval.

Sociologists of course viewed delinquency as a distinctly urban problem, symptomatic of poverty, overcrowding, and other perils associated
with the large city. Not coincidentally, juvenile delinquent fictions followed suit. Novels published after the war were generally consistent with
the American reformist tradition — big-city narratives superficially reminiscent of Crane's *Maggie*, Dreiser's various tragic melodramas, Wright's
Native Son, and especially Farrell's *Studs Lonigan*, the work that best captured the milieu of the urban jungle through its reliance on authentic language and realistic detail.

But the teenagers depicted in books that emerged in the 1940s about
rebellious youth were more alienated, more cunning, and a more dangerous and violent breed than any that had emerged from the pages of previous fiction. Still, the substance of earlier classic literary productions from
which juvenile delinquent fiction was derived was largely diluted by a
spirit of almost solemn purpose to both diagnose the moment, and, as the
genre evolved, to project its realities into prophecy.

The ephemeral nature of the genre to produce quickly and for profit
also made its creators inclined to make the moment of perception slave to
audience expectation. Geoffrey O'Brien correctly defines the eclecticism
and timeliness of the novel of juvenile delinquency.

> It was a curious phenomenon that seemed to creep out from
> under the prevailing genres of the day creating its own audi-
> ence as it went along. The juvenile delinquency novel had one
> great advantage in that it could effortlessly be all things to all
> people, social tract directed against hoodlums, cowboy story,
> pornographic novel in which all sex could be justified in the
> name of naturalism, and finally a subversive hymn of praise to
> the delinquents themselves, to be enjoyed by the same audience
> that flocked to see Marlon Brando in *The Wild One* in 1951.[1]

But the juvenile delinquent novel also had another purpose. While
addressing the general horrors unleashed by headstrong youth, it nonetheless pronounced to its readers that the effect of delinquency on a domi-

nant culture was negligible and reassured that all was well. Delinquency, it was suggested, was only an aberration caused by the war or by fading historical factors and was, given certain adjustments, like any other disease, ultimately curable.

One of the earliest and most traditional novels of the genre was Willard Motley's *Knock on Any Door* (1947). Ostensibly a novel of social protest, the book details the moral deterioration and eventual death by execution of Nick Romano. It is Nick's early reform school experience in Denver and Chicago that turns him against all authority and ultimately leads him to murder. Losing his faith in traditional values because of the loss of his father's grocery store and a subsequent plunge into poverty, Nick aspires to imitate unsavory role models such as Tony, who teaches Nick how to steal; Vito, who shows Nick how to exploit drunks and homosexuals for profit; and eventually Ace, a mobster for whom Nick later works.

Nick's decline is, as the novel's title suggests, inevitable. In an attempt to make his character as sympathetic as possible, Motley launched an unqualified attack on society and a detailed look at the process of corruption of innocence as vitriolic in its wrath as Richard Wright's *Native Son*, the novel that *Knock on Any Door* most closely resembles. Motley even includes a long speech by trial lawyer Andrew Morton characterizing Nick as social victim in a manner similar to that of Boris Max, who appeals to the court to spare Bigger Thomas's life.

Yet Motley missed the sense of transformation and power that radiate from a demonic figure like Bigger, who insists on personal responsibility for the act of murder, his desperate gesture to achieve identity. Forgoing a rejection of Max's sociological pleadings like the one made by Bigger, who prefers to embrace the existential nature of his own cruelty, Motley instead graphically presents the gruesome execution ritual, glimpsing at the last minute reflections of the jury members who pronounced the young man's fate.

Motley's polemic is thus preserved but not without occasional intimations of glamorous defiance that enliven the dreary proceedings, particularly in Nick's narcissistic posturing, understood as necessary attributes to hustling and petty crime, and in his motto, "live fast, die young and have a good-looking corpse."[2] If these are strong words for a protagonist who lacks both an ethical center and a commitment to a life of crime, they might indeed be appropriate for the next wave of juvenile delinquent fiction.

Irving Shulman's *The Amboy Dukes*, also published in 1947, was a far more typical example of the genre, though like Motley's novel it too was indebted to a classic literary predecessor — James T. Farrell's *Studs Lonigan*. Shulman incorporated from Farrell the tragic waste of potential that his main character, not innately evil, possesses. Sixteen-year-old Frank Goldfarb has ambitions to be an accepted member of the Amboy Dukes, his neighborhood social club, but, like Studs, Frank has certain moral standards not necessarily shared by his streetwise peers. For instance, Frank refuses to participate in a gang rape of an old prostitute and objects when the boys try to steal her earnings; he helps Fanny Kane after she is raped and beaten by Crazy Sachs; when he and Benny accidentally kill their shop teacher in a struggle for a zip gun, Frank insists on reporting the incident to the police (he eventually blunders into a confession); he confides in the slum-bred athletic director Stan Alberg, who is eager to reform young Frank; he despises Crazy Sachs for his senseless, vicious violence and resents the Dukes' unqualified acceptance of Crazy.

To some of the Dukes Frank's gestures toward decency betray a failure of nerve — "we ain't got room in the Dukes for guys with crap in their blood,"[3] says Larry Tunafish when at first Frank is reluctant to smoke marijuana. Yet Frank's misgivings are not in essence due to a lack of courage; at times he distinguishes himself as a formidable warrior, especially in a poolroom fight with Mexican gang members that Frank starts. And he shows bravery in his being constantly antagonistic to the dangerous Crazy Sachs, "a street and gang fighter spoken of respectably.... Crazy might draw a knife and begin slashing" (29). It is Crazy, in fact, who kills Frank at the end of the novel by flinging him from a rooftop. Nonetheless, it is Frank's independence and courage of conviction that result in his not being completely accepted by the Dukes, and he eventually becomes a distrusted outsider.

Farrell's portrait of Studs Lonigan shows a divided, confused character who adheres both to the tough code of the street and to the contradictory standards of Irish Catholicism that Studs is careful to conceal from the gang. Frank, on the other hand, is in true revolt against his family and social circumstances, not just a helpless teenager assaulted by evil forces and succumbing to them. Reservations about the extremes or the efficacy of some gang activities do not prevent him from aspiring to be an exemplary gang member. Frank is a classic tragic figure, transformed by his circumstances but nevertheless contributing to his own sad destiny: "he had moved into the world of boys who seemed to live at a hysterical pitch of

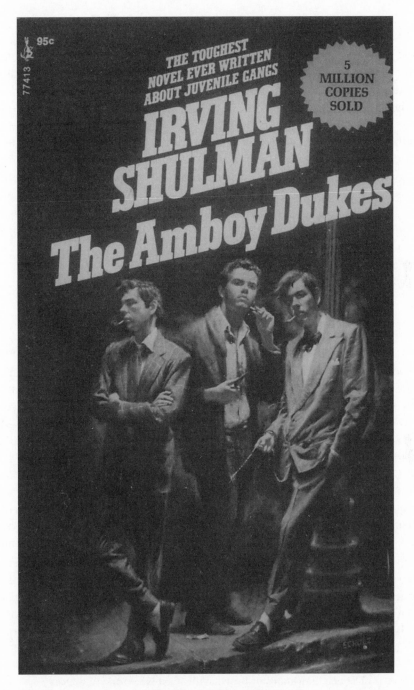

The Amboy Dukes, Pocket edition, 1971.

excitement" (11). This, Shulman suggests, is a young man's unfortunate alternative to a bland social reality characterized by inept and sanctimonious teachers like Stan Alberg and the hopeless poverty and thankless laboring of his parents.

Yet Shulman's novel is most interesting in its flashes of an emerging subculture, the energies of which are caught mostly in matters of style and attitude, the main defenses of the disaffected young.

> The boys were careful of their dress, and since it was late spring they wore pastel tan, blue and brown gabardine suits, three-button jackets, ticket-pocket, center vent, deep pleated trousers with dropped belt loops, pegged from twenty-four inches at the cuff. Sharp. They wore open-collared sport shirts, and their ties were tied neatly in broad knots. Nonchalantly they swung long key chains that hung from a right or left belt loop, and the keys spun in continuous enlarging and contrasting circles. The boys sported ducktail haircuts: long, shaggy, and clipped to form a point at the backs of their heads. Their slick Vaselined hair shone in the reflection of light.[6]

The threat to authority in much of *The Amboy Dukes* is provided by a conscious cultivation of image and style by the gang members. Shulman shows that the lifestyle is adult, as if the gang members, bereft of a childhood existence or of rites of passage to a better life, need to grow up quickly but on their own terms. Unfortunately, such a revolt aims merely at self-promotion: the implications of a true revolt that could transcend cultural and civilized authority have not taken shape. Thus the Dukes may dig the subcultural fetishism of the wild rhythm and blues played by the cool band at their club-sponsored dance, but the creators of orgiastic expression are themselves not respected, not perceived as purveyors of something truly valuable; the Dukes plan not to pay the band members and to beat them up if necessary. Mad Monk and his Cats are notably black; hence racist motives take precedence. In addition, as in all activities the gang members pursue, satisfaction of immediate impulses is imperative, the consequence of which is usually an incitement to further mindless violence. Shulman's novel capitalizes on and frequently replays scenes of gratuitous, self-destructive violence that serve to restrict teenage threat to the confines of urban locales.

> The neighborhoods of Brownsville, East New York, and Ocean Hill were infested with gangs. The Pitkin Giants, the Amboy

> Dukes, the Sutter Kings, the Killers, the D-Rape artists, the
> Zeros, the Enigmas, the Wild-cats, the Patty Cakes were just a
> few of the gangs that fought, slugged, and terrorized the neigh-
> borhood. They fought for the sheer joy of bloodying and maul-
> ing one another, and no insult was so slight that it could not be
> used as an excuse for a mass riot and free-for-all. (46)

Because the alienated teens are unable to find fulfillment or self-
knowledge through subcultural activity, their behavior largely reflects the
corrupt adult world, and the gang protest is therefore ultimately incoher-
ent. Military codes, oaths of loyalty, and protection of territory grounded
in narcissism and conceit are the operatives and major catalysts of gang
violence. Shulman's narrative cancels out the subversive power of gangs
by showing how empty they are of real countercultural dimension and
how easily gang members may succumb to the limitations and self-destructive nature of their revolt. Similarly, Sol Yurick, in his novel *The Warriors*
(1965), would explore the political, not the cultural, implications of youth
revolt and also characterize it as a ridiculous failure.

The Amboy Dukes, like many other novels of its type, plays the fantasy of an adult society visiting retribution on the nonconformist young,
and it is direct rebellion against adults that provides most of the tension
in the novel. The book is notable for its many instances of adult-adoles-
cent interaction, most of which show gang members at first as formidable challengers to authority. "These kids aren't criminals yet, and we can't
find holes in their alibis ... they're getting wilder and tougher every day
(112) opines a worried cop. Nevertheless, in every case the authority of
youth revolt is undermined by the fact of its systematic defeat. The novel's
plot centers on the cat-and-mouse battle between the police investigating
the murder of the shop teacher and the two who are responsible, Benny
and Frank. The accomplices are certainly victims of youthful distrust of
each other, but more important, they succumb to skillful pressure applied
by the police. Illusions of solidarity, loyalty, and bravery — virtues central
to gang survival — are thus destroyed. Even a seemingly insignificant scene
conveys the inadequacy of teen revolt. Feivel, an ex-professional boxer
employed as a houseman of the Winthrop Billiard and Recreational Par-
lor, where the boys shoot pool and hang out, is respected by most gang
members because of his glorious past, but he is inevitably challenged to a
fight by a member of the Tigers. Though he is momentarily a worthy opponent, the boy is soon roundly defeated.

Time and again in *The Amboy Dukes* juvenile delinquents are crushed by adult authority, physical strength, or greater wisdom, all of which reveal generational conflict and show youth subculture tarnished and weakened by adult intervention. Still, with the exception of Evan Hunter's *The Blackboard Jungle*, rougher treatments than Shulman's were emerging — quickly paced novels with stylized violence, providing more allegiance to prurient interests than to sociology or prophecy.

Duke (1949) was the debut novel of New York City social worker Hal Ellson who, along with Shulman, Wenzell Brown, Edward DeRoo, and a number of other forgotten authors, became something of a specialist in this type of fiction; *Tomboy*, *Rock*, and *The Golden Spike* were all novels with violent teen protagonists. *Duke*, with a sale of 1,540,000,[4] was a big success and substantially contributed to the growing popularity of the juvenile delinquent genre. Like most novels of its kind, its popularity was largely due to its ghetto setting (the protagonists were always dispossessed Jews, Blacks, or Puerto Ricans), which distanced a readership of Americans — many of whom were comfortably settling into suburban housing developments — from the threat of teen revolt both by social circumstances and by ethnic difference.

Duke, the main character of the novel, is the black, fifteen-year-old president of his gang The Mighty Counts. Unlike Frank Goldfarb, who is led into a life of evil because there are no influences to lead him into good, Duke ostensibly embraces the vile actions for which he is forced to take responsibility as leader of his warlike group. Ethical values, which debilitate a character like Frank Goldfarb, are left out of the novel, thus eliminating the struggle between good and evil.

Yet in some ways Duke is no less aimless a drifter than earlier protagonists, at times willingly engaging in the power he possesses as a leader, while at others trying to escape it, though this is due not to social breakdown but to mental imbalance. "I was a nutty cat," says Duke, and it is this premise to which the novel offers its major concern and development. Duke is an insomniac who detests his race and various physical irregularities of his own, especially his nose, which he finds ugly and wants to "chop off," and his tiny hands, which he believes "are getting smaller all the time. Sissy hands."[5] In addition, Duke believes he is being pursued by a one-legged man, he hears voices, and he sees faces coming out of his bedroom wall. Given Duke's various activities as drug runner for Juan, a local pusher, and as incessant pot smoker, his suspicion of police observers is perhaps not unexpected, nor would his slum environment, which creates ennui and lack of self-worth, be an unlikely factor in producing neurosis. Ellson's first-person narrative, however, blurs any relation between social evil and mental deterioration; Ellson was clearly more interested in chronicling the extent of Duke's madness and corruption than in locating its source.

In addition to calling the shots for his gang, which usually requires taking violent action against rival gangs like the Kings and the Skibos, Duke is a pimp supervising a brothel, a dope pusher, a rapist, a thief, and possibly a murderer. His extreme ruthlessness is displayed during the robbery of a drugstore as Duke complains about the small amount of money taken in the heist. "There was only twenty-five in it. That got me mad. I went in the back then and talked to the old man. He got it in the mouth with the gun butt. I bashed him and he gave up twenty more. Then he started to make some noise so I had to quiet him. He got tapped on the skull." (112) Moreover, gang fights in *Duke* are not typical hand-to-hand fracases accompanied by makeshift weapons, or chains, pipes, or knives, but usually shoot-outs or ambushes with revolvers — this contrasted with the Amboy Dukes, who possessed shop-class zip guns not known for their accuracy and carried mostly for show. With all sense of moral proportion removed from his novel, Ellson cultivated his excesses and achieved a genuinely bizarre pop surrealism.

Sensitive to charges of sensationalism, Ellson claims in a prefatory note (a staple of the genre defending itself against charges of pornography or glorification of teen violence) that his novel "was not written to glorify evil."[6] Yet despite Ellson's moral indignation and sociological pleadings, his kinky portrait of a ganglord paralleled the outrageous cover art that became the most memorable characteristic of the genre. Ellson's novel was the first internal view of the juvenile delinquent, one that was largely unrestricted by sociology and the manipulation of archetype, and became the prototype of the kind of ultraviolent juvenile delinquent fiction that went on the attack when youth culture occupied the attention of the masses during the 1950s.

Evan Hunter's *The Blackboard Jungle* (1954) also represents an inside view, but this time it is the view of one who is presumably in a position to do something about juvenile discontent. Yet, the travails evident in the attempts of a Bronx vocational schoolteacher to improve the prospects of economically marginal teenagers through education provides scant hope for solution within the novel's own terms. Hunter's novel, while not showing youth subculture directly, as in Shulman, or from the inside, as in Ellson, does little to vitiate the persistent belief that there is nothing inspiring in the prevailing institutions of society.

The main character of *The Blackboard Jungle* is an idealistic young teacher, Rick Dadier, first-year employee at North Manual Trades High School. Despite his efforts to reach students, he is continually frustrated. A World War II navy veteran, Rick brings a combination of amiable level-headedness and smooth regimentation to his English classes, strategies that fail miserably. His students are crude and vulgar, answering his questions with rude quips and referring to him as "Mr. Daddy-O." His attempt to meet their hostility with relative nonchalance backfires on him the first day, and after engaging in witless repartee with a belligerent student, Rick "could not think of a comeback, and rather than spout something inadequate he fled behind the fortress of his desk."[7]

But Rick's efforts are eventually redeemed when his students come to his aid after he is wounded in a classroom knife fight with Artie West, a vicious, psychotic youth and the novel's chief villain. This eventual student collusion with the enemy teacher, however, is not unprepared for. Earlier in the novel Rick supervises the annual Christmas play in which several of his students, including Gregory Miller, a gifted young black student and the typical good-boy-gone-wrong-gone-good, participate. Throughout the Christmas play section of the novel, Hunter makes it clear that despite maintaining a pose of indifference or hostility in class, these students betray an affable other face in different circumstances. Hunter thus emphasizes the mere posturing that accompanies petty hostility and rebellion that is suspended during moments of truly sinister behavior like Artie West's. Violence is in fact kept to a minimum save for the demented actions of Artie, whose hatred for Dadier is so great that he sends threatening letters to Rick's pregnant wife, causing her to miscarry. The novel also includes a rape scene, which accounted in part for its reputation as a potboiler and its subsequent popular success.

But if Hunter convinces us that most students are not the violent rebels they pretend to be, one is not convinced that their lot will improve. The novel leaves the impression less of a dedicated teacher's victory against almost impossible odds than of overwhelming corruption, a clear picture of a useless, decadent institution — the trade school — which, notwithstanding a fluke conversion or two of some of the more reasonable souls to good judgment, can only continue to produce despair and cynicism.

Part of the problem stems from the hostility and indifference of the administration and of Rick's fellow teachers. The administration, speaking from strict standards of discipline, exercises a fascistic control over both teachers and students. Criticized for having used terms like "nigger," "spick," and "kike" as negative examples to teach a lesson in democracy, Rick stands his ground on principle but reflects afterward: "That's a hell of a way to do things, he thought. Drag a man in on the carpet and accuse him of being a prejudiced sonofabitch without ever having heard his side of the story. That's a truly democratic way of handling things, all right.... What do I have to do, fight the kids and the teachers?" (212)

Moreover, the teachers have grown indifferent and cynical. Rick classifies teachers as "clobberers," those who "reciprocate hostility with physical force"; "slobberers," who appeal to the sympathy of the boys; and "slumberers," who "treated discipline as a non-existent problem ... he thought, and if no one heard what he was teaching, it was just tough ... the slumberer's philosophy was a single one: let the bastards kill themselves, so long as I'm not hurt" (212).

The chief spokesman of the slumberers is Solly Klein, veteran teacher whose cynicism shocks Rick and threatens his idealism. "I'll tell you something, Dadier. This is the garbage can of the educational system. Every vocational school in the city, you put them all together, and you get one big, fat, overflowing garbage can. And you want to know what our job is? Our job is to sit on the lid of the garbage can and see that none of the filth overflows into the street. That's our job" (201).

As Rick's resolve to reach the students who don't care wavers, he adds a new class of teacher to characterize himself — "the fumbler," who "simply didn't know what the hell to do. The fumbler kept trying. He tried this way and he tried that way, and he hoped that some day he would hit upon the miraculous cure-all for the disciplinary problem" (201).

What he does hit on of course takes the form of physical bravado, a display of force in which superior strength as well as sheer courage — not intelligence and understanding or academic breakthrough — produces the desired effect.

The Blackboard Jungle is an angry indictment of the urban trade school, revealing that not only are proverty and lack of opportunity major causes of urban decay and wasted lives, but the institutions themselves, rotten and disintegrating at their very foundations, are major contributors too. Despite such condemnation, there was comfort in knowing that it was possible to isolate a source of youthful disaffection just as there was momentary triumph in recognizing that the alienated teen is not so alien, just another conformist.

Many of Hunter's angry attacks on urban education were also voiced in Paul Goodman's nonfictional *Growing Up Absurd* (1956). But Goodman, a sexual libertarian descended from Wilhelm Reich, added a primal element to his analysis of rebellious youth, diagnosing violence as a consequence of repressed sexuality that he believed "would drive them to more frantic excitement to break through."[8] Goodman was also critical of a society that rewards those who master role-playing for the sole purpose of maximizing financial profits rather than attending to the human needs of youth. According to Goodman, "the system pre-empts the available means and capital; it buys up as much of the intelligence as it can and muffles the voices of dissent; and then it irrefutably proclaims that itself is the only possibility of society, for nothing else is thinkable."[9]

The most damaging result of this meaningless perpetuation of the status quo and its empty value for Goodman is that it creates cynicism in those best suited to achieve worthwhile goals, placing them outside the community. Sympathetic to the youthful victims of an inadequate and corrupt system, Goodman wonders "why the grownups do not more soberly draw the same connection as the youth"[10]—that is to say, at least to recognize the utter absence in our society of useful, rewarding activity. Goodman, however, is as critical of those who substitute one useless activity (senseless gang violence and rebellion) for another (aspiring to achieve ignoble conventional goals), both of which are expressions of conformity and lead to oblivion or mediocrity, be it through self-destruction or anonymity.

Goodman proposes an adversarial response to easy acquiescence, promoting a kind of existential engagement with orthodox culture, though he is unclear as to how this intelligent rebellion would be manifested in an overpopulated technocracy. Goodman rejected the Beats, who had just emerged at the time, interpreting their drug taking, wanderlust, and mysticism as social irresponsibility, and, like juvenile delinquency, reflecting a drop-out mentality. To live inside yet to reject roles imposed by society was for Goodman the only sensible response to the numbing, socially ossified atmosphere of the fifties in America.

Goodman's utopian vision was a tall order indeed, one that demanded an unusually high level of creativity in the face of the overwhelming realities of cultural ignorance and self-serving institutional resistance. But despite Goodman's somewhat sanctimonious moralism, a mode that characterizes juvenile delinquent fiction too, his analysis of youth problems and his accurate observations of new expressions of cultural hostility taken by those who were breaking away from mainstream life signified a new intimacy and sensitivity to the situation. Juvenile delinquency was still considered a social problem, but some new novels that appeared exhibited a sudden and unexpected sympathy for the adolescent individual. Moreover, their creators resisted condemning teenagers who fail to conform to predetermined patterns of socialization and avoided stereotyping by showing the struggle of the young to overcome alienation. This direction, probably owing something to the questing nature of Beat writing and to a clearly emerging youth culture, can be seen in Harlan Ellison's 1958 novel *Web of the City* (originally published as *Rumble*).

Ellison is a cult figure whose appeal for his readers has always been a strong intimacy with his characters, the intensity and directness of his writing, an adherence to social consciousness, quirky choices of subject matter, and an eclectic, often whimsical overlapping of literary genres. *Web of the City* avoids both pop conservatism and the familiar cant of social protest by refusing to implicate society too heavily in the misguided deeds of his characters or to conform to the prevailing cultural prejudices of the genre. Instead, Ellison asserts the value of individuality and social responsibility as ways of dealing with one's oppressed circumstances.

The tensions in the novel exist between the violent life of juvenile crime and the desire of one of those criminals to escape it. Rusty Santoro, former leader of his New York gang, the Cougars, has ambitions to break away, but the gang won't let him. Only loyalty counts, a condition that makes it almost impossible for him to achieve his goal. Much of the novel is devoted to Rusty's reluctant self-defense against his old gang members who harass him. But being forced to take defensive measures increases his psychological conflicts; Rusty is undergoing the acute identity crisis of someone who does not fit in.

> As he crouched there, without even knowing it, he was reliving all the times he had stood with a zip in his hand, and faced another boy. At times like that, just as this time, he felt like speaking some other language than English. Was it his native Spanish, a tongue he had never really spoken — never really appreciated — a third generation Puerto Rican seemed so

irretrievably lost to that slim heritage, or was it some other language? Perhaps it was the growl and scream of the beast. Did
the jungle call to him at those times. After all, wasn't that what
he was reduced to when he fought?[11]

This juvenile delinquent hero, a jumble of identities given complexity by ethnic and psychological factors, sets out on a quest to establish a
responsible self, and this action becomes the central issue of Ellison's novel.
Yet the terms of liberation and self-discovery are problematized by the
force of the city itself, which Ellison chose not to treat naturalistically but
in extravagant metaphors suggested by the title.

Ellison's science fiction of the sixties was revolutionary in its program
of departure from early pulp origins and their reliance on made scientists,
gelatinous monsters, and menacing aliens from outer space for story material. But in *Web of the City*, Ellison's imagery is drawn from precisely such
sources. The city is anthropomorphic, mechanistic, paralyzing human will,
"a black widow which cannot stop weaving,"[12] inhabited by parasites like
Boy-O the junk dealer, Candle Shaster, Emil Morales, and Beast.

Eventually, the novel shifts its focus from alienation and mechanistic
evil to revenge. In a final scene recalling the conclusion of *The Amboy
Dukes*, Rusty tracks down Beast, the killer of his sister, and gets retribution by letting him plummet to his death from the roof of an apartment
building. The novel finally attests to violence as being an organic part of
life in the city, an eternal truth for all who dwell there and preventable
only through escape.

Despite *Web of the City's* shifting thematic center, metaphysical pretensions, overwrought prose, and uneven mixture of allegory and realism,
Ellison's novel did indeed move the genre to new ground. On its surface
the novel seems typical, focusing as it does on an adept though reluctant
warrior engaging conflict in all the familiar urban settings like amusement
parks, bowling alleys, subways, open lots and tenements. But notwithstanding its fatalism, *Web of the City* is the story of the teen with problems and not of "the teen problem." As the sources of social injustice
faded, what was left was the search for uniqueness central to the existence
of most teenagers, a quest that Ellison, unlike most writers of juvenile
delinquent fiction before him, chose not to deny.

But in spite of the perception that even a good kid could express frustration through violence, most writers of the genre continued to deal
unsympathetically with youth. Indeed, as youth culture finally arrived in

the fifties as a force to be reckoned with, the attack grew stronger. Perhaps the biggest fear had finally emerged with the arrival of Elvis Presley, the white man as black, who exemplified sexuality in his musical expression but who even more directly showed that the root component in teen culture was explicitly a black one, in fashion, music, speech, and attitude. Such had been hinted at in *The Amboy Dukes*, but after the emergence of rock and roll, "violence-crazed" and "brutal" were the usual adjectives used to describe the sorry state of youth.

A 1957 anthology, *The Young Punks*, collected stories from leading writers of the genre, including Evan Hunter and Hal Ellson, but the urban settings were largely rejected in favor of more neutral ones such as the beach, where a girl is murdered by a juvenile crazy, or the open road, where a family is pursued and terrorized by a gang of punks. But as violent as these formula crime stories are, Leo Margulies's introduction to the book reveals better than any fiction could the truly hysterical response to youth culture.

> These kids are tough — and what are you going to do about it! Here are knife-carrying killers, and thirteen-year old street-walkers who could give the most case-hardening call girl lessons in how to hold their clients. These kids pride themselves on their ethics: Never go chicken — finish whatever you start, even if it means knifing your best friend in the back. Never rat on a guy who wears your own gang colors — unless he rats on you first. Then he's just a punk. When you feel the urge to be "real gone" coming on you, don't resist it, even if it means shooting down a cop. Old men on crutches are always fair game, but it's all right to help a chick you've taken a fancy to over a mud puddle in the street. If she starts playing you for a sucker — blacken both her eyes and walk away fast.[13]

The exposure of gang codes was of course long familiar from the novels, but what is new here is a disaffected rhetoric, its truculence no longer veiled by sociological pleadings.

Perhaps it was inevitable, given the political dimension of the juvenile delinquent genre, that the true range of the threat represented by teen revolt would be explored. Sol Yurick's *The Warriors* (1965) was the inevitable climax and the novel to end all novels of juvenile delinquency. Written at a time when protest against the Vietnam War began to take shape, when racial strife meant black people taking to the streets, and when

The Young Punks, Pyramid edition, 1957.

violent anarchy seemed a real possibility in America, *The Warriors* dramatized a challenge mounted by the vast numbers of young dispossessed of New York.

Ismael, a parody of a militant black nationalist, leader of one of the city's most powerful gangs, calls a meeting in a park of representatives from New York's toughest street gangs. A momentary truce declared, the multitudes gathered before him, Ismael reveals his plan to upset the old balance: "He told them about the dream he had. One gang could, in time, run the city. Did they know what a hundred thousand was? There were only about twenty thousand fuzz. Why should the biggest power force, one hundred thousand, in the city be put down by the Enemy and the Other?"[14]

But to achieve his dream Ismael realizes that solidarity must be established among numbers of youths who have lived out their lives in conflict with each other; he must nullify hostilities and persuade other gang members that his vision is possible: "'Now we're all brothers ... they made us think we're all different so we rumble as colored gangs, Puerto Rican gangs, Polish gangs, Irish gangs, Italian gangs, Mau Mau gangs. But the iron fist breaks all our heads in the station house the same'"(37).

Of course, the elements of racism, hatred, the psychotic impulse towards senseless violence, lack of discipline, and fear of an opposition that had conditioned the gangs to tremble in the face of such a challenge are too strong and must quickly shatter any coalition of his kind. Fights eventually break out between gangs, and Ismael is killed by a stray bullet.

So much for any organized challenge to authority. The rest of the novel depicts the struggle by members of the Dominators, one of the gangs present at the gathering, to return to their Coney Island turf. Their journey is complicated not only by the presence of police anxious to arrest gang members for the chaos that had erupted at the meeting but by rival gangs whose territory they must inevitably traverse to get home. In addition, they lack weapons to defend themselves, left at home to accommodate terms of the truce, and their leader, Arnold, has been killed. Thus the significance of the epigraph to the novel taken from Xenophon's *Anabasis*, which recounts the march of a Greek army numbering ten thousand men from Babylon to the Black Sea after the death of their leader at the Battle of Cunaxa — "Soldiers you must not be downhearted because of recent events. I can assure you that there are as many advantages as disadvantages in what happened."[15]

However, Yurick's focus on members of the Dominators — Junior,

Lunkface, Dewey, Hector, Hinton, and Bimbo—does not in any way illustrate the heroic qualities of the gang. On the contrary, Yurick wants to expose in detail that the cowardice, stupidity, and recklessness that characterize the large mass applies to every individual gang and gang member. The Dominators, in fact, demonstrate none of the qualities essential to warriors. At first safe in hiding in a cemetery after Ismael is killed, they leave their hiding places because they are afraid that the corpses will come out of their graves. Their first solution to the problem of getting home is to call their youth worker to pick them up in his car. They remove their gang insignias in order to become inconspicuous to rival gangs as they pass through enemy territory. They engage in practically no confrontations with other gangs but instead challenge each other to senseless contests to determine their manhood, the winner being the one, for example, who can urinate the farthest from the subway platform edge. And the nearest they get to the gallantry of Greek warriors is the comic book that Dewey carries with him; as he reads he fantasizes about having exploits like the heroes in the comic who march through deserts, over mountains, fighting enemies often and defeating them.

Yurick's main strategy is thus irony. When Hector, the gang's second leader, Bimbo, and Lunkface are arrested after trying to rape a drunken nurse, leadership falls to the most sympathetic character, Hinton, who is sensitive and intelligent, a teenage Odysseus, more the clever survivor than the fearless warrior. Having returned to Coney Island with junior and Dewey in tow, Hinton is elated that "he had become the Father" (153). Yet this is a hollow triumph because Hinton returns to his mother's apartment, which he calls the Prison, met by the hot, smelly atmosphere of poverty. There he sees "his mother, Minnie, fat, perspiring in the stuffy sweat and baby-pissed air ... being fucked by her man" and, engaged in similar activities, his sister and her junkie boyfriend, Alonso (158). The novel ends with Hinton trying "to tell Alonso about the family and what it meant, and how they had gone through so much that night" (154), while Alonso, failing to understand, prepares a shot of heroin.

The hopelessness of Hinton's situation, however, does not negate the sincerity or the veracity of his explanation. Yurick's novel is most effective as a novel of the city, evocative of a dense, indecipherable place. As Hinton's journey dominates the latter part of the novel, the city's dark topography is revealed through his zeal to survive as he travels underground in subways, concealing himself in alleys and brothels to avoid apprehension.

Hinton does indeed arrive at long last, a kind of hero, having escaped his foes with intelligence and craft rather than by Xenophon's methods of democratic leadership. Yet Yurick reinforces Hinton's tragedy by showing his delusions, his insistence, like that of all the Dominators, on fantasy to make his grim life bearable. Hinton is not even particularly rebellious and longs for a normal life, to marry, have a job, and raise a family. Because this is an unlikely prospect, the gang becomes the surrogate — a thing to belong to. The attempt to transform an unsatisfactory reality into something favorable is given major focus in a long, drawn-out scene in which Hinton gratifies himself by shooting down a cowboy sheriff in an arcade, all imagery borrowed from the movies, one more vicarious pleasure in a dispossessed world.

Unlike the combat novel, with its legalized violence, exotic setting, and its insistence on revealing the inner workings of the new man, the novel of juvenile delinquency was limited by its formal responses to the seemingly inexplicable actions of America's youth. Most products were undistinguished because of their ambivalent connection to both subject and audience. The authors of this fiction provided a formal critique of a "social problem," which, by necessity, required them to stand above youth rituals from a cultural vantage point outside those rituals. Generally self-righteous in analysis, the juvenile delinquent novel moralized its way into oblivion. Genuine insight was rare as a result, and it never captured the youth audience to whom it would most appeal. As teen culture became marketable, pop novels suffered. O'Brien points out that "there was no way they could do more than trot along behind the movies, the music, the television images, trying none too imaginatively to capture some of the magic for their own profit."[16]

By the late fifties the juvenile delinquent mystique reached a certain self-conscious climax in film and drama. *Rebel Without a Cause* and *West Side Story* diluted the sociology and emphasized the romantic side of their alienated teen characters. The result was tremendous commercial success. Thereafter, a series of exploitation films appeared — cheaply made quickies produced by schlockmeisters like Sam Katzman and Albert Zugsmith, both of whom made careers out of cashing in on trends like juvenile delinquency and rock and roll. American International Pictures was also in the teenage exploitation film business, releasing at least twenty juvenile delinquency films during the 1950s.[17] By 1960 the string was played out, eventually being replaced by biker and beach movies.

But during the heyday of the juvenile delinquency craze, a more appropriate response to social anxiety was on the horizon, one that the confused and contradictory products of the juvenile delinquency genre were incapable of articulating and one that, being literary in nature, did not need to do battle with other popular art forms that it would have a hand in transforming.

3

Hipsters, Beats, and Supermen

As the naturalism of Dreiser, Wright, and Farrell metamorphosed into the routine melodramas of underprivileged youth in the juvenile delinquent novel, the genre created an energy all its own, particularly in its graphic and sensational subject matter and in its lewd cover art iconography. But the new cultural transformation was no illusion, not one simply manufactured by writers of potboilers, eager paperback entrepreneurs intent on exploiting postwar disaffiliation, or liberals attempting to reform society. Indeed, these tales of sexuality, drug use, violence, and tribal ethics signaled a new immersion in a primitive ethos and constituted a most significant forerunner to future rituals of liberation in American fiction. Notwithstanding the intentions of their authors, these tales of slum environment and agonized destiny were early chronicles of escape into alternative forms of community and organized defiance of rational principles.

John Clellon Holmes described the pervasive atmosphere after World War II as "a feeling of expectation without reasonable hope, of recklessness without motivation, of uniqueness seeking an image."[1] While Holmes might be characterizing any number of juvenile delinquent heroes, he is more specifically referring to older (though still young), more introspective victims of social change. These seekers, however, were attracted to programs of self-indulgence more as rites of passage to spiritual affirmation than as terms of denial and disillusionment.

One important transitional work, serving as a middle ground between juvenile delinquent fiction of the forties and the Beat novels of the fifties, was J. D. Salinger's *The Catcher in the Rye* (1951). Holden Caulfield's rejection of a commercialized and materialistic society echoes the similar inclinations of juvenile delinquent and Beat misfit heroes who rage against a society whose values seem decadent or misplaced. But, as suggested by this novel's steadfast popular appeal since its first publication, Salinger's innocent and sensitive young protagonist is more representative of all adolescents who feel at odds with the adult world than he is a clear barometer of the malaise that pervaded the culture during that precise historical moment.

The restlessness and spiritual longing referred to by Holmes was expressed more accurately in various Beat chronicles throughout the 1950s. Jack Kerouac's first novel, *The Town and the City* (1950), though ostensibly recounting the postwar dislocation of a family, symptomatic of various social, cultural, and institutional breakdowns, contains within it what was probably the first glimpse of the underground. The most relevant section of the novel reflects Peter Martin's experiences in New York City. Observing the strange, desperate activity of Times Square, he perceives "all the cats and characters, all the spicks and spades, Harlem-drowned, street drunk and slain, crowded together, streaming back and forth, looking for something, forever moving around."[2] Yet Peter is more than just an observer of the scene and forms an alliance with the community of urban hipsters, including Leon Levinsky, Will Dennison, and Junky, aliases for Allen Ginsberg, William Burroughs, and Herbert Huncke respectively. This section of the novel closely parallels Kerouac's own New York experiences in the late 1940s.

There were other documents of the phenomenon. In 1949 Anatole Broyard's "Portrait of a Hipster" appeared in *Partisan Review*. Broyard himself would become, as Henry Porter, the focus of Chandler Brossard's *Who Walk in Darkness* (1952). The novel, a roman à clef, was typical of most early Beat fictions, especially in its portrayal of the ambivalent, voyeuristic relationship between a first-person narrator and a charismatic, amoral other. A critique of the new bohemia in Greenwich Village during the early fifties, the novel's ambiguous moral tone and its focus on the new sensibility set an important standard. Ambiguity results from the novel's flat documentary style, which recalls Hemingway, especially in its scenes of boxing matches, parties, and the blossoming of a love affair in a world that is falling to bits. The existential drift, however, unaided by those codes of behavior that mark Hemingway's aristocrats of the soul, creates a compelling situation that captures emerging Beat consciousness.

Blake Williams, an unemployed writer, tells his story with the detachment of alienation from meaningful activity. A social drifter, Blake, like most of his associates, explores the street milieu of coffee houses, seedy bars, and village loft parties. Blake is referred to as "the arrow collar man of the underground" and a "part-time hipster,"[3] only peripherally connected with this darker world, flirting with its chaos as an extension of his own.

Blake remains a peripheral figure throughout the novel because he does not share the values of the world he sometimes inhabits. Evidence of this emerges as he tells the story of Henry Porter, hipster par excellence, for whom the narrator's admiration turns to hate and disgust. Porter is presumably a black man attempting to pass as white, a distinction that deepens his sense of mystery for everyone. In addition to mystery, the attraction-repulsion factor keeping Porter's fellow Greenwich Village wanderers in his company seems to be a certain adeptness at adjusting to new circumstances in a world cut off from an older sense of morality and value. This quality of detachment — a crusade to be cool by avoiding feeling — is reflected in Porter's antiromantic view of love ("why should there always be that sentimental crap in a relationship? ... a piece if a piece") and in his world-weary cynicism ("Everybody is out to save himself. I've never seen it fail").[4]

By contrast, Blake's values are conventional enough, despite his abstract psychological nausea and the matter-of-fact surface of his narrative. He is in love with Grace, Porter's girlfriend, toward whom Porter is of course indifferent, a fact that infuriates Blake. Pregnant with Porter's child, Grace gets Blake to find her an abortionist, and Blake helps her through the painful aftermath. Porter, an extraordinary heel, is eventually rejected by Blake and his friends, and a return to old-fashioned feeling and personal commitment is the hoped-for antidote to the nihilism of the moment as the lovers, who are "so tired of everything being reduced to a kick,"[5] contemplate a liaison. It is this element of self-righteousness that led Delmore Schwartz to comment in his review of the book that "the hero is engaged in showing how most of the human beings he knows are evil while he is good."[6] But while Harry Lees, Blake's best friend, lies dying in a hospital, the victim of a beating by teenage hoodlums, insulation from the underground is made to seem an uncertain prospect.

Curiously, the option of cool is not entirely rejected. There is little profit, the narrator understands, in exploring one's feelings, which obviously leads to neurosis in his case, and even less profit in demonstrating them: "Nobody was going to help you not to be lonely, and I knew — lying there listening to that grinding up of refuse — that the more you showed your loneliness the less people wanted anything to do with you."[7]

Brossard's novel has often been called the first Beat novel, but the author has rejected any Beat associations on the basis of its sober, realistic, antiromantic view of the hipster scene.[8] Brossard prefers to call his novel one of the first works of the *Nouveau Roman*. Indeed the novel is mostly surface realism, though its gestures to French literature seem more accurately reflected in the narrator's sense of unreality as revealed by his neurotic reflections, a psychological complexity more indebted to traditional realism than to Robbe-Grillet. The book's reputation, by contrast, whether Beat or not, lies in its more typically American distinction of renovating and disrupting content through the presentation of activities — jazz, pot smoking, and social codes of aloofness — that had previously been untreated in serious fiction.

John Clellon Holmes's *Go* (1952), the first novel to include the term "Beat Generation" (Kerouac used the term "Beat" in his first novel), a greatly underrated book, is similar to Brossard's in its detached, voyeuristic ambiance. Paul Hobbes, the narrator of *Go*, is another skeptical observer of the dark world of New York bohemia. But while alienation and nihilism are central metaphors of the spiritless age that Holmes describes, Holmes's novel gives full range to the particulars of the quest to find meaning. Possibilities for transcendence are located in three characters, all representing aspects of the Beat credo to be developed through subsequent novels — David Stofsky (Allen Ginsberg), who frequently sermonizes on the spiritual, visionary way out; Gene Pasternak (Jack Kerouac), who pursues the simple pastoral life; and Hart Kennedy (Neal Cassady), who celebrates hedonism and the Dionysian life of intuition and motion. Throughout, however, Hobbes remains a reluctant convert to any of these solutions. In an analysis of Stofsky and Pasternak, Hobbes reveals his ambivalence:

> The two of them often amazed and irritated him. They poked into everything; they lacked a necessary self-doubt, that extroverted subjectivity that Hobbes was accustomed to and accepted without criticism.
>
> They made none of the moral and political judgments that he thought was essential; they did not seem compelled to fit everything into the pigeonhole of a system ... they never read the paper, they did not follow with diligent and self-conscious attention the happenings in the political and cultural arena;

Go, Appel edition, 1977.

> they seemed to have almost calculated contempt for logical judgment; they operated on feeling, sudden reaction, expanding these far out of perspective to see in them profundities which Hobbes was certain they could not defend if put to it.[9]

Stofsky's eccentric mysticism is emphasized in the novel. The formulation of spiritual principles is given expression by Stofsky's willingness to suffer all the pain of experience — it is Stofsky who gets involved most deeply in criminal activities, getting arrested after participating in a stolen property scheme — as well as to alter consciousness to find the true essence of reality at a deeper level of the psyche. Stofsky's road is visionary, selfless, questing, insisted on after he hears the voice of his literary hero, William Blake, his own words echoing the master — "the way to salvation is to die, give up, go mad! ... to suffer everything to be: to love ... well, ruthlessly" (109).

Gene Pasternak is more moderate in his ambition, and of all the characters in the novel he is most like Hobbes himself. Through Pasternak Holmes defines the tensions that threaten to further engulf the questers of urban bohemia: "Pasternak's life seemed to turn into a battle against the city itself. But the city was an opponent invisible because it was impersonal. It could not be beaten by a single man, and sometimes the only alternative to strangulation seemed to be to cheat it, by escaping" (55).

Pasternak's locus of escape is pastoral, not mystical — "I want to get out in the country some place, lots of land and big ranches" (55), he says. Pasternak disappears later in the novel to go on the road but reappears at the end, presumably unfulfilled.

Hart Kennedy represents the third possibility of salvation through intense engagement with life, though the solution to alienation he offers is harshly dealt with. Kennedy is characterized quite vividly as an opportunist and exploitation artist, possessed of "shrewd, masculine ugliness" (114), and Hobbes is unable to share his friends' unhealthy attachment to Kennedy or their admiration for his restless energy. Hobbes especially despises the need of these early Beats for a leader, an exemplary figure, and appropriately employs military images to describe the dangers of hero worship. "Moving down Forty-Second Street in a restless platoon, they darted into bars and coffee stands and penny arcades, Hart deploying them with enthusiastic commands" (119). Hobbes is also critical of Kennedy's lengthy monologues with their insistence that one can dig everything all the time by virtue of an unqualified sense of wonder, the quality that

Kerouac admired most about Cassady. Hobbes responds with "annoyance at the idea, because to him everything was not really true. There were some things, and some ideas, that were seriously false" (145).

But Hobbes, as unsparing as he is in his negation of pretension and futility, is probably most critical of himself. There seems to be little value in maintaining distance between himself and the magnetic hipster culture building up around him and in which he travels, or, as Stofsky tells him, of "Looking down on everyone in a secretly patronizing way like a mass observer who never forgets his job even when he participates" (152). The vehicles engaged by others, though short-circuited, at least give them the capacity to feel something other than despair. Hobbes, an Apollonian among Dionysians, lacks this capacity.

Hobbes's attraction to the bohemian circle seems grounded in a yearning for the innocence he believes they possess. Thus, despite the accuracy of his observations, his ability to see the illusory shortcomings of every situation, Hobbes wants to cast off his cynicism and be more like them.

Yet Hobbes's gestures of friendship (to which Pasternak best responds) and his immersion in Beat activities (smoking marijuana, listening to jazz, being open-minded about promiscuity even to the extent of not protesting when his wife has an affair with Pasternak) are negated by his despair, which he shares with another Beat character named Agatson. But unlike Agatson, a demonic wreck of a man who celebrates self-destruction and dies an absurd death in a subway accident at the end of the novel, Hobbes experiments with danger only tentatively. He creates situations that result in his progressive erosion of spirit and alienation from others. The "new" ranges from frantic self-assertion (Stofsky, Pasternak, Kennedy) to cool detachment (hipster cool, familiar from Brossard and seen in Hobbes's analysis of the cool man in the bar). Both forms of alienation are disdained by Hobbes because for him both frantic activity and enforced reticence ultimately lead to the extinction of the self. Hobbes prefers instead to cling to a depraved version of the self that is reinforced by correspondence with Liza, a neurotic young college student from Columbia. In these letters Hobbes tries to enact an exalted and solitary sense of suffering, a feeling made less acute by Beat insistence on community and by the constraints necessary to maintain a stable marital relationship with his wife Kathryn. Hobbes's progression to despair climaxes in the dingy, graffiti-covered men's room of a waterfront bar in which his self-examination leads to a confrontation with the void, and ultimately to a final epiphany:

The sense of freedom in his life, the idea of being able to control it, direct it, even waste it, of being able to entertain certain fancies that were detrimental or exercise a volition that was dangerous; all these suddenly seemed to him to have been the most shameless illusions all along, the idiotic industry of an ant building his hill in the path of a glacier, and imagining that he was free [281].

Hobbes's suffering has led to a transformation of sorts, a vision of waste based on the folly of his own experience and the experiences of his friends. Thus Hobbes rejects loveless isolation but not for the communal, mystical, or ecstatic standards proposed throughout the novel. Instead, Hobbes asserts the value of personal connection, suggested by his reconciliation with his wife.

For Holmes, who, like Brossard, felt more acutely the chaos and not the community of the new bohemia, there was reward in learning that madness and death were not mere abstraction voiced by mystical prophets like Stofsky but alarmingly real possibilities and thus undesirable solutions to the pervasive spiritual malaise. For Jack Kerouac, a much more idealistic and intuitive writer but one sharing Holmes's honesty and oppositional goals, it took absolute immersion in experience to arrive at similar conclusions. To a deeply introspective writer like Holmes, romantic escape into pastoralism, Blakean vision, meaningless energy, and male bonding were unacceptable solutions to urban despondency. Yet, with energies played out in an urban landscape, enlargement of purpose and quest were the next logical steps in the underground odyssey.

Drawing on his working-class background, a personal optimism and openness to experience derived from Thomas Wolfe, and archetypal myths of the road given expression previously by Whitman and London, Kerouac created the central and still most important fictional work of the Beat Generation. *On the Road* (1957) went further than any of the earlier hipster novels by setting forth the idealism based on a new way of life and hence a way out of cultural and spiritual dislocation. *On the Road*, characterized by a rapid-fire prose style and a corresponding optimism periodically darkened by gloom prompted by glimpses of the limitations of the ideal, is a calculated and extremely self-conscious account of the new ethic.

On the Road was a significant break from the city novel and its urban nightmare associations, though in previous Beat novels urban isolation and

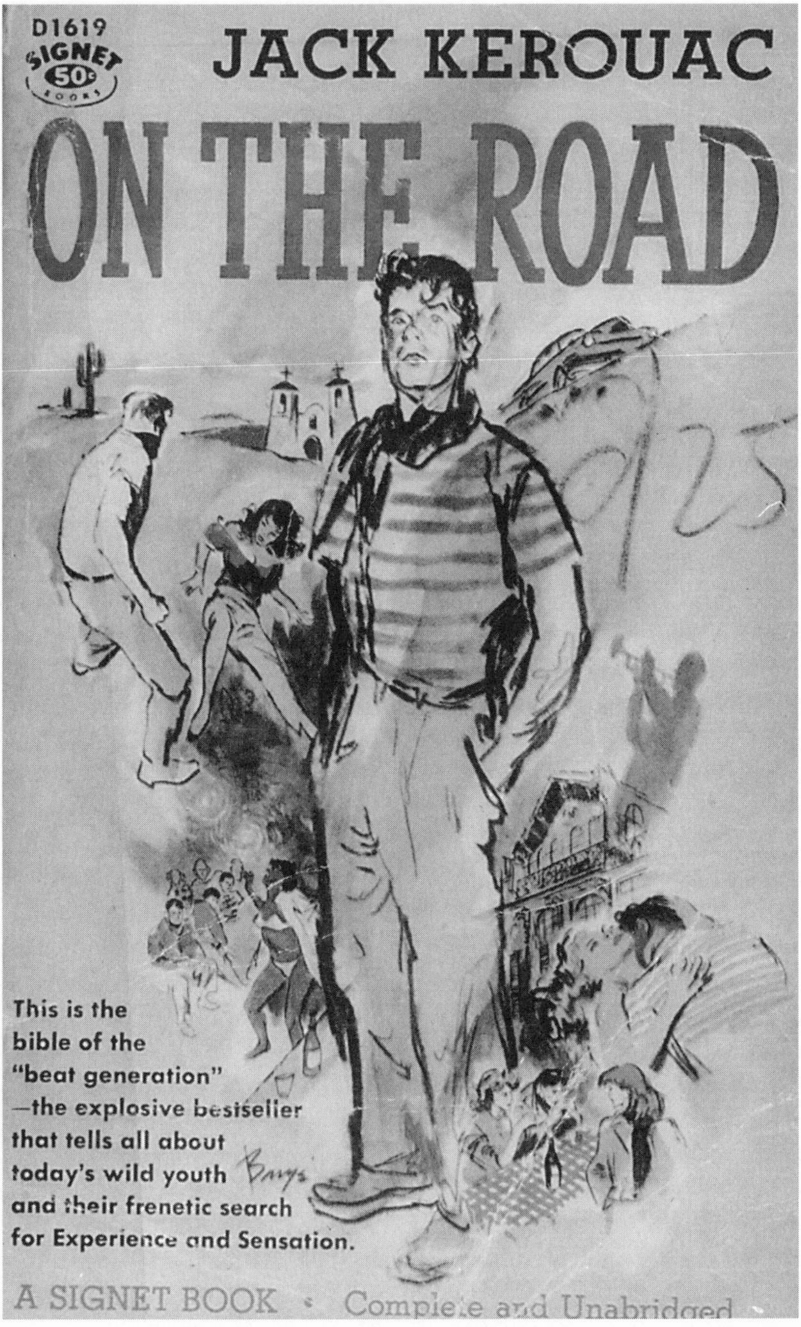

***On the Road*, Signet edition, 1958.**

narrative distance characteristic of naturalism had been removed; as the displacement disappeared, the reader was exposed more and more to areas of life hitherto unexplored. Sal Paradise thus embraces the mysteries and excesses of life provided by trips to Mexico, San Francisco, Los Angeles, Denver, and New York. In these settings the novel moves away from areas that are systematically stifling — from east to west, from civilized to primitive — and it is within more remote environments that primal connection and strangeness are seen as promising vehicles to psychic and spiritual recovery.

Early in the novel Paradise has an affair with a Mexican girl, Terry, with whom he hitchhikes to California and with whom he becomes a fellow migrant worker. While picking cotton, Paradise reflects, "I was a man of the earth, exactly as I dreamed I would be."[10] He even registers a vicarious confirmation when he learns that he is being pursued by Terry's spurned husband and his Mexican friends: "They thought I was a Mexican, of course, and in a way I am" (97). But Paradise is not adept at picking cotton and is unable to provide for Terry and her child. As gloom, misery, and poverty become increasingly hostile to the continuation of their love affair, the narrator reveals how ill-suited he is to that world. "I could feel the pull of my own life calling me back" (98). Paradise leaves her soon after.

Such scenes, in which reality, exhaustion, or geography impose on the process of redefinition, recur in the novel with great frequency. Sal Paradise often acknowledges the emptiness and ennui inherently peculiar to his journey and that can only be resolved by more frantic activity — travel to a new place. San Francisco, one of Sal's haunts, is another land of promise, but it too signifies an end both thematically and geographically, his progress to transcendence suspended in a state of confusion. Thus endless parties crash, as in the New York novels of Brossard and Holmes, their participants victims of physical exhaustion and a ruptured sense of community. Other "paradises" sought by the narrator offer glimpses of transcendence but simultaneously signal his alienation from the source. At the end of the novel, traveling through the Mexican mountains, Paradise contrasts the primitive purity of the natives with his own tainted knowledge bred of a corrupt civilization. Begging for money, the Indians

> had come down from the back mountains and higher places to
> hold forth their hands for something they thought civilization

58

could offer, and they never dreamed the sadness and the poor
broken delusion of it. They didn't know that a bomb had come
that could crack all our bridges and roads and reduce them to
jumbles ... our broken Ford, old thirties, upgoing American
Ford, rattled through them and vanished in the dust [299].

But while the journey away from civilization, away from one's past,
creates an eventual impasse, Kerouac kept the pessimism which is pervasive in Holmes and Brossard from violating the generally positive tone of
his novel. Though Sal Paradise's journey is a frustrating one, or at least
one that turns back on itself only to begin again, it is nonetheless the
process of the journey itself that accounts for most of the book's power.
Supported by its informal procedures and a nonreflective exuberance, *On
the Road* is finally less about tapping the potentialities of the present than
it is about creating a mythology from past events.

In *On the Road* Kerouac captured, as he never would again, the fresh-
ness of the experience with the immediacy of revelation. "That's the West,
here I am in the West" (21), beams Paradise at one point with youthful
amazement. In Kerouac, immediate transformation, regardless of dura-
tion or fulfillment, is important. In Denver, for example, Paradise attends
a performance of Beethoven's opera *Fidelio* and comments ironically,

> "Only a few days ago I'd come into Denver like a bum; now I
> was all racked up sharp in a suit, with a beautiful well-dressed
> blonde on my arm bowing to dignitaries and chatting in the
> lobby under chandeliers" [52].

Sal Paradise thus remains a divided character, like Kerouac himself,
responding to the stimuli of the moment, subject to periods of confusion
and elation, and torn between bourgeois values and transcendent ones.
What prevails is an overwhelming sense of wonder. Uncritical of the events
recorded, Kerouac nonetheless showed the virtue of not detaching himself — of not constructing a defensive analysis like Holmes. Kerouac rejected
adult skepticism in favor of returning to the alternating fears and ecstasies
of childhood. As Michael Davidson has said, "It is this essentially boyhood
state with its large-scale projections of danger, magic, power, and innocence that characterizes much of Kerouac's own work."[11] In addition, while
Kerouac's book shows the limitations of self-indulgence in ecstatic wanderlust, it fulfills the need of the questers of Beat faith for a hero.

The real subject of *On the Road* is Dean Moriarty (Neal Cassady):

holy primitive, con artist, cowboy roughneck, seeker of experience in any form, and most important, an archetype for the natural, transformed new man. It is Moriarty's presence that allows the narrator to transcend the tone of existential uncertainty that characterized Beat chronicles before *On the Road*. Kerouac's novels increasingly reflected a tragic sense of life as the novelist peered deeper into the limitations of the ideal and his romanticism unraveled. But with Kerouac's optimism located in Moriarty, who embodies the freedom that the narrator can never achieve, the novel is given a center and a passionate energy that its episodic and impressionistically fragmented methods would otherwise obscure. Paradise's sketchy character is thus presented for functional reasons, as the worldly adept Moriarty and the innocent neophyte Paradise are contrasted. Through Moriarty, Paradise is shown the folly of rationalistic and materialistic impulses that reflect the dominant culture in favor of a more instinctive spiritual orientation.

The precondition, of course, must be that Paradise possess few of the qualities that make Dean Moriarty such an admirable figure. Moriarty, for example, like the Mexican innocents in the mountains, like Terry and many other primitives worshipped throughout Kerouac's narrative, possesses the special knowledge. Walking through the streets of Denver searching for Dean, Paradise wishes he were a "negro, feeling that the bed the white world had offered me was not enough ecstasy for me, not enough life, not enough joy, kicks, darkness, music, not enough night," and confesses that all his ambitions, especially writing, were "White ambitions, that was why I'd abandoned a good woman like Terry in the San Joaquin Valley."[12]

It is of course Dean, "who knew these streets so well from childhood" (180), the hipster exempt from convention and able to preserve the vital primitive response, who truly has the courage to embrace life on the edge and survive. The need to reflect on experience and to record it is not shared by Dean, who is always able to get beyond the spiritual impasses felt by the narrator. The novel concludes with Sal's illness, an apt metaphor, which comes at the point of near transcendence in Mexico, while Moriarty goes on, abandoning his friend for more life.

At the novel's conclusion Paradise is indeed critical of Moriarty's insensitivity and disloyalty, yet this does little to discredit Dean's heroic status. Moriarty's negative qualities are alluded to from time to time in the novel but they are usually dismissed in favor of a positive portrayal.

Hipster amorality, manifested in a disregard for the consequences of one's actions, was of course the source of Holmes's and Brossard's uneasiness with the hipster figure. Neal Cassady, basis of the Moriarty character, was an ex-con, thief, liar, con artist, and hustler when Kerouac met him in 1946, and Cassady's abandonment of friends, family, and his generally criminal behavior are often alluded to in *On the Road*. Moriarty is manipulative, says Paradise, because he "wanted so much to get involved with people who would otherwise pay no attention to him" (195). Later, he defends Dean as being misunderstood, or accuses others of being envious of Sal's "position at his side, drinking him in as they once tried to do" (195). What is clear is that Kerouac's attempt to present Moriarty as religious prophet, avatar of pure being, a new kind of hero obscured Moriarty's demonic side and resulted in the narrator's unwillingness to gauge his megalomania.

Kerouac saw with greater clarity than any of the Beats the potential of creating a version of the outcast rebel to affect cultural change, even though it was Allen Ginsberg who took greatest advantage of the countercultural explosion that took shape a decade later and that Kerouac rejected. Kerouac's main strategy in *On the Road* was to blur the relationship between fact and fiction, thus implying that the impact of the new man was spiritual and cultural. *On the Road* was, allegedly, a record of an important development in a cultural process, not literary artifact, and its author was more passive recorder than he was the inventor of it.

It is well-known that Neal Cassady was not pleased with Kerouac's portrayal of him in *On the Road*, that he felt betrayed, and publication of the novel practically ended their friendship. While this in itself cannot attest to the accuracy of Kerouac's portrayal of Cassady, nor should it matter in a work of fiction, one may nevertheless conclude that the mentor-neophyte relationship between the two men was largely exaggerated. Sal Paradise's major illumination in the novel is his ability to recognize "IT" — a transcendental moment in which the complete essence of something is understood. Dean illustrates this concept by referring to the bop players they had seen the previous night. "'Now, man, that alto man last night had IT — he held it once he found it, I've never seen a guy who could hold it so long.' I wanted to know what 'IT' meant" (206). Kerouac, a veteran of the Village scene if the forties and impassioned and knowledgeable jazz listener, as well as writer about jazz back to his Horace Mann days,[13] was no neophyte in such matters. But the culturally revolutionary effects of his novel were calculated primarily to give Cassady emphasis as cultural savior, not the author.

Kerouac's cultural project was further enhanced when he attributed his stylistic breakthrough — his much-vaunted spontaneous prose — to Neal Cassady himself, alluding to letters he had received from Cassady in the late forties as the source. However, Cassady's only published efforts — his unfinished autobiography *The First Third* (1971) and selections from his letters to Kerouac, including a fragment of the lost "Joan Anderson" letter — actually betray little influence on Kerouac's novel. *The First Third* is characterized by a stiff mixture of formal, self-consciously literary language with awkward lapses into colloquialism, and his letters by a more direct but still undisciplined voice, almost always about Cassady's sexual experiences or personal disasters such as lost jobs or broken marriages or about stealing cars or hitchhiking.[14] Kerouac's prose, on the other hand, is inhabited by a consistent voice, committed to an effort to give the essence of the emotion or subject while at the same time avoiding conventional novelistic patterns. Kerouac's intentions were best summed up in a plot synopsis of *On the Road* for Frank Morley. He called the book "an imaginative survey of a new American generation known as the 'Hip' (The Knowing) with emphasis on their problems in the mid-century 50s and their historical relationship with preceding generations.... This new generation has a conviction that it alone has known everything, or been 'hip' in the history of the world."[15]

Yet, despite Kerouac's attempt to create a cultural explosion and at the same time an enduring work of American literature, it would be a writer with analytical talents beyond Kerouac's to give the new phenomenon clear definition. It was Norman Mailer, in his iconoclastic essay "The White Negro" (1957), who best articulated the quality of amorality that the Beats were fascinated by. Moreover, Mailer established the political dimension of the hipster, which also eluded the Beats, and recognized the locus of the hipster's power in violence and anarchy. Of course many of the elements were already familiar from Beat writing; Mailer, for instance, focused on the importance of action and the existential nature of immediacy — the "changing reality whose laws are remade at each instant by everything living, but most particularly man, man raised to a medieval summit where the truth was not what one felt yesterday or one expects to feel tomorrow but rather truth is no more nor less than what one feels at each instant in the perpetual climax of the present."[16] Mailer also incorporated Beat tenets of ecstatic motion into his essay: "Movement is always to be preferred to inaction. In motion a man has a chance, his body is warm, his instincts are grist."[17]

But Mailer's essay gave larger scale and anarchistic dimension to the hipster revolt. Taking his cue largely from a fractious analyst named Robert Lindner, whose theories of the criminal psychopath were best expressed in his book *Rebel without a Cause* (1944),[18] Mailer advocated expression of one's desires as a means of attacking the source of neurosis — the society that created it: "Hip proposes as its first tendency that every social restraint and category be removed, and the affirmation explicit in the proposal is that man would then prove to be more creative than murderous and so would not destroy himself."[19] Like Kerouac and Beat novelists before him, Mailer found in the underground milieu the vitality that he sought. Yet Mailer accepted the risks that accommodated dangerous self-affirmation. His inclination to promote the violence subliminally supporting the underground revolution rather than mute or reject it was grounded in the enormity of the challenge. To Mailer the goal of the struggle was not simply to break from bourgeois middle-class values, as in Beat literature; it was a fight for the very soul and psyche of the human organism — the stakes were high. Moreover, Mailer's ready acceptance of violence was grounded in his wartime experience. The underground was the extension of the combat platoon, the subterranean world defined by risk and aggression, unseen and alienated from the presence of authoritarian power.[20]

While many of Mailer's observations might characterize a hipster like Dean Moriarty, his own sense of the hipster differed radically from Kerouac's so that the demonic aspects were enlarged and given scale and authority rather than explained. Mailer, in fact, in "Hipster and Beatnik: A Footnote to 'The White Negro,'" attempted to clarify the crucial differences between hip and beat. He saw the Beat as mystical, contemplative, middle-class, revolting against his parents so that "he can feel moral value in his goodbye to society." He is "torch-bearer of those all-but-lost values of freedom, self-expression, and equality which first turned him against the hypocrisies and barren cultureless flats of the middle-class."[21]

The hipster, on the other hand, is less sentimental and desires to change reality rather than escape it. For the Beat, who "contemplates eternity" and exercises adversarial options by withdrawing, the path of liberation through violence and psychic release is unappealing. The biggest difference, however, is political; according to Mailer, the Beat is usually a liberal, but the hipster "looks for power, and in the absence of radical spirit in the American air, the choices of power which will present themselves are more likely to come from the Right than from the moribund liberalities of the Left."[22] If Mailer, like Reich before him, attacked Freud because it was the purpose of psychoanalysis to tame the power of the rebel, he attacked liberalism because political liberation abrogated the differences among men and engendered cultural mediocrity.

Mailer's attack was no less than a full-scale assault on the humanist tradition. After the villainous Sergeant Crofts in Mailer's first novel, the vehicle for this attack found expression in the ruthlessly self-conscious hipster Marion Faye in *The Deer Park* (1955), whose purpose it is to get beyond morals and sin. His existence a concentrated "effort to beat off compassion, Faye knew all about compassion. It was the worst of vices ... once you knew that guilt was the cement of the world, there was nothing to it; you could own the world or spit at it. But first you had to get rid of your own guilt and to do that you had to kill compassion."[23]

This project to erase the moral conscience is attempted through Elena, the woman whom Faye sadistically dominates and whom he tries to coax to suicide, "finally the situation where he could push beyond anything he had ever done."[24]

Faye falls short of purging himself of compassion, but his story is continued in "Advertisements for Myself on the Way Out" (1958), a fragment of a projected longer work. Again, Faye is possessed of "that exquisite terror of sensing oneself at the edge of secrets no other being has been brave enough to invade,"[25] and he is still obsessed with destructive impulses — this time the murder of a friend as a means of achieving an authentic private reality.

Mailer did not actually test his thesis that murder can be part of an attempt to cure a diseased soul until his 1965 novel *An American Dream*. If Marion Faye's quest to get beyond guilt seems a bit too cerebral, a theoretical testing of boundaries that does not always reveal the true seriousness of the actions he contemplates, Stephen Rojack, hero of *An American Dream*, is assailed by the full implications of everything he does, including the murder of his wife, Deborah, and in all its legal and spiritual consequences. Rojack's multilayered consciousness reflects a hero who is both self-assertive and self-deprecating and who constantly abandons himself to situations in which he may be fully possessed by power or powerlessness, magic or dread, God or the Devil.

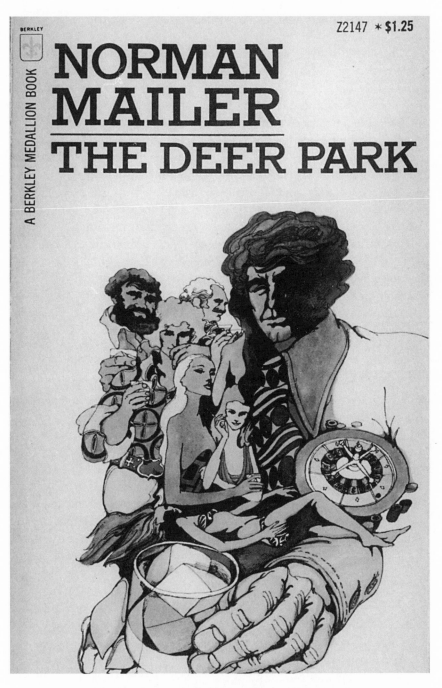

The Deer Park, Berkeley-Medallion edition, 1967.

The world of the novel, a New York City charged with mystery and hallucination yet familiar enough in its depiction of places like the Waldorf Towers and of Harlem cold water flats, also expresses a coexistence of opposites. In this Manichean universe, where privilege and power meet the risk-taking hipster, Mailer imbued events with levels of intensity quite beyond their literal setting, much as D. H. Lawrence did in *The Rainbow*, to establish significance beyond the surface. Nevertheless, unlike Lawrence of *The Rainbow*, Mailer flaunted his own presence in the novel. It is hard to ignore the Rojack-Mailer connection in characterization — intellectual, war hero, wife stabber, media celebrity — or in the action of the novel as it shows Rojack thriving in both the underground world of Cherry and Shago Martin and in the corporate power nexus of his wife's father, Barney Oswald Kelly, or in Mailer's grand literary gestures, which Leo Bersani has said reflect the "natural tone of a man for whom events have become strictly literary-novelistic situations to be freely exploited for the sake of a certain style and the self-enjoyment it unexpectedly provides."[26] Diana Trilling also has observed that much of Mailer's writing reflects an "impulse to break the metaphor barrier and himself act out, or ask that we act out, his idea."[27]

Mailer's project has been to get beyond merely reporting the strategies of the underground to subvert control or to enact an independent existence, the main activity of most underground writers. In a civilian world where a context for direct and meaningful conflict between the controlling forces and the underdog has largely been removed, Mailer took great pains to include authoritarian sources as presences in his fiction. Thus, after *The Naked and the Dead*, in which the army is portrayed as a destroyer of humanity, a harbinger of more radical oppression to come, Mailer located forces of control in the bureaucratic agents of *Barbary Shore*, in the Hollywood of *The Deer Park*, and in the powerful social economic-political conspiracies of Barney Kelly in *An American Dream*. Mailer did not shrink from identifying the aggressive new powers he saw assailing American society, warning as did another important social commentator of the postwar period, C. Wright Mills, that as the domains of economic, political, and military power become "enlarged and centralized, the consequences of its activities become greater."[28]

The hipster combined the searching virtues of the bohemian and the violence of the juvenile delinquent with the vital underclass black culture. But Mailer's hipster-existentialists remained solitary figures — individualists confronting the horrors of a larger society, as well as a dark personal self. Ken Kesey's version of the new man emphasized, like Mailer's, the Nietzchean qualities of the hipster, enlarging the dimension of the Beat hero and the range of his powers. In addition, while Beat writers before Kesey were content to depict an authentic if shocking view of the underground, Kesey, like Mailer, showed the rebel in confrontation with the oppressor. But given a greater sense of urgency and human community and reinforced by Kesey's willingness to fully embrace the Beat ethos, Kesey's new Beat hero was, despite movements towards anarchy, more consistent with Kerouac's use of the hipster as galvanic agent of cultural change than with Mailer's desperate quest for freedom and salvation.

Still, allowing for certain allegiances to Beat archetypes, the barriers to transcendence that inhibited Kerouac, as evidenced by numerous frustrations to breakthrough found in *On the Road*, are nonexistent in *One Flew Over the Cuckoo's Nest* (1962). Kesey's nonconformist supermen promised not simply liberation from evil and injustice but, as the psychedelic era unfolded, a pathway to group consciousness and unrestricted power.

Kesey has acknowledged the enormous influence of Kerouac's novel on his own narrative. Like *On the Road*, which deals in a central polarity between movement and stasis, *Cuckoo's Nest* focuses on the opposition between madness and sanity. Kerouac's road was allegorical, a quest for salvation that prevented the civilized man from achieving transcendence. The road offered escape and momentary liberation but remained an abstract adolescent dream, its promise eroded by time, personal conflict, and memory. *One Flew Over the Cuckoo's Nest* is no less allegorical, but its setting of a ward in a lunatic asylum is, ironically, a more liberating place than Kerouac's endless road. Kesey sought to find liberation within the context of restriction. He needed to transcend the problem of geography by turning inward, locating change in the internal life, in chaos, madness, and anarchy, the final possibility.

All Beat writing was a search for liberation and affirmation of life, but Kesey went farthest in the solutions and methods required to effect change. Kesey's willingness to explore the barriers of rationality and to test the power of madness went beyond Kerouac's flirtations with that subject, though it was Kerouac again who provided the influence. The agent of change in Kesey, as in Kerouac, was the new hipster, the madman and hustler. But Kesey's notion of "IT," the goal of the hip quester, was not so much a Buddhist-like moment of ecstasy and vision as it was a more lasting radical transformation of consciousness.

Kerouac's relationship between neophyte Sal Paradise and mentor Dean Moriarty has its parallel in the relationship of Chief Bromden and Randall Patrick McMurphy. Unlike Paradise, however, who falls short of transformation by virtue of his need to observe and by his inability to actually be Dean Morarity, Chief Bromden is indeed radically transformed. Kesey's masterstroke was to register the change of consciousness in the narrator himself. It is the chief who is most radically affected by McMurphy's presence, an achievement given sufficient weight by the length of his incarceration and by the extent of his psychic withdrawal not just into meek neurosis but into complete silence. Moreover, while McMurphy's antics affect everyone in the novel, Chief Bromden dramatically projects McMurphy's influence by engaging the most radical action — breaking loose from the confinement of the asylum.

Yet it is also true that such extreme change is possible because of Chief Bromden's divided nature. A half-breed, he is cut off from his true self, partially defined by the white world that has domesticated him, his inhibitions generated by a white mother representative of an enfeebling white civilization. Ironically, Kerouac's self-division proceeded from a white middle-class background he longed but failed to break from and to which he ultimately returned, more specifically to the domesticating mother.

Chief Bromden's narrative is more vision than quest. Throughout the novel the chief experiences an uncovering of his past, his forgotten values, and more importantly, his true self. This recognition is gradual; at the beginning of the novel the chief is completely cut off from any sense of himself and his roots.

> I hide in the closet and listen, my heart beating in the dark, and I try to keep them from getting scared, try to get my thoughts off some place else — try to think back and remember things about the village and the big Columbia River, think about one time ah Papa and me were hunting birds in a stand of trees near Dallas.... But like always when I try to place my thoughts in the past and hide there, the fear close at hand seeps through my memory.[29]

Significantly, the chief responds to McMurphy as does no other inmate because he recognizes his repressed renegade self in the other man. In the novel's terms, madness is preferable to sanity; the inmates of Nurse

Ratched's ward are ideal conformists for the main portion of the novel. In fact, Kesey makes it clear that except for the chronic cases, these patients are not really mad at all. They are volunteer patients, not formally committed to the asylum. The ward is of course a prototype of the world outside, controlled by technology and authoritarian repression intended to weaken the inmates and allow Big Nurse to sustain control. What is needed is courage to transcend the boundaries she sets, and Kesey thus assigns grandeur to the demonic and destructive.

As the chief becomes less inhibited by psychotic withdrawal symbolized by fog machines and by his ability to withstand the effects of electric shock treatments, a clearer picture of McMurphy emerges, less mythical, less idealized. This view reveals Murphy to be crazier than was previously suspected, sometimes aware of the stakes of the game he is playing against the system and sometimes not.

In addition, McMurphy's mission of salvation to liberate the asylum's inmates from the Combine by generating a collective action, getting the patients to stand on their own without help, which most sympathetic critics perceive as being central to the novel, is called into question. Self-centered McMurphy asserts the value of the strong man, as manipulative not only of the systems he intends to smash but of the men who are unwilling victims of the system. Detached from and superior to the spectacle of the ward, McMurphy is a master of deception and exploitation. Myth making is imperative, not reform. Time after time McMurphy dupes and exploits the patients for his own gain — making a profit on the fishing trip, besting them in wagers, and constantly winning at cards. And he suspends such calculations only when he is moved to act on impulse, as when he assaults the orderly Washington, or in his near-rape of Big Nurse after Billy Bibbitt's suicide. Otherwise, McMurphy continues to tread the line, confident that he will go unpunished, testing the boundaries of power in a generally self-serving manner. As Chief Bromden, a most unreliable narrator, interprets the meaning of events as he sees them, it is clear that the chaos McMurphy generates precludes the crusade for liberation that the chief often attributes to him. For most of the patients, liberation from constraints is unfeasible, and they cannot follow, as their betrayal of McMurphy at the end shows. But as McMurphy submits to the chaos of the party at the end of the novel and fails to escape by falling asleep, ultimately being lobotomized as a result, he becomes an inevitable martyr and liberator in the chief's eyes.

As schematic as Kesey's novel is, particularly in its neatly arranged oppositions between machinery and nature, order and disorder, repression and liberation, Kesey created an uneasy relationship among elements. Thus the Christ myth (McMurphy as savior) and archetypal American myths such as pastoralism and Indian blood consciousness create thematic balance in the novel (Kesey's fiction, unlike Kerouac's and much other underground fiction, is well-crafted) but ultimately ring false. The chief breaks out of the system hoping to return to his origins by making a journey back to his tribe on the Columbia River. But Kesey's attempt to impose a pastoral denouement on the novel obscures the terms in which he imagined a breakthrough — through inner vision, through ego, and through disorder.

Kesey wanted to impose a metaphor on his material to reflect his transcendental message, yet at the same time he needed to show the manifestations of his novel's themes in terms of real, meaningful action. Though the chief's return to his tribe is problematic, Kesey at least wants us to believe that Chief Bromden has exceeded McMurphy in terms of power. McMurphy's hat won't fit the chief, and he realizes that he is physically bigger than McMurphy.

Kesey, like Mailer, was becoming impatient with literature and would play with the possibilities of his proposed inner liberation in communal terms. Yet ultimately, for Kesey, who played the roles of megalomaniacal autocrat and, later, isolated individualist to the hilt, even repudiating the drug culture, which he had played such a central role in creating, it seems that liberation could best be achieved in terms of individual experience. Perhaps this explains why Kesey's books are all projections of the author himself — grand contemplations on power and its use in the world.

Leslie Fiedler has said,

> We have come to accept the notion that there is still a territory unconquered and uninhabited by palefaces, the bearers of "civilization," the cadres of imperialistic reason; and we have been learning that in this territory certain psychotics, a handful of schizophrenics, have moved on ahead of the rest of us — unrecognized Natty Bumpoes or Huck Finns, interested not in reclaiming the New World for any Old God, King or Country but in becoming New Members of just such a New Race as D. H. Lawrence foresaw.[30]

The underground narrative in the postwar period attempted to define the new man in the terms in which he lived and thrived. Kesey's vehicle to personal and cultural transformation after suspending his writing career was LSD, a temporary departure from the world of reason, assisted by the Merry Pranksters, over whom Kesey played the lordly guru. Acid and the journey of the painted day-glo bus was a refinement of Kerouac's quest, the inner movement blending with the outer, come full circle with arch hipster Neal Cassady at the wheel.

The Beat novel was a remarkably coherent phenomenon, each a progression beyond the previous one, each a further experiment in liberation from traditional literary constriction and from the mores of the dominant culture. Each novel reached farther to attempt to define more precisely a cultural process.

An additional purpose was to identify the antinomian impulse and to encourage its expression in each of us. But what began as a project of cultural democratization soon took on apocalyptic implications, challenging the tenets and moral sanctions of the humanist tradition. Rejection of the values of one's culture led to the creation of underground heroes devoid of any values at all and reflecting many of the same dangerous urges as the political enemies against whom they battled. For authors not comfortable with such dangerous vehicles of liberation, other areas, hitherto invisible aspects of America, remained to be explored.

Breaking the Last Taboo:
The Gay Novel

A superficial look at the gay novel might suggest that it was part of a general trend in postwar literature to liberate the word from Puritanical restraints so that writers would be better able to confront sexual activity frankly and honestly. Though writers who explored the homosexual underground took advantage of new tendencies that by the sixties allowed them to better represent the world of the homosexual subculture, the truth is that they were not pioneers in this trend; they were, in fact, an initially somewhat divided group, renouncing the standards of straight society and yet paradoxically insisting on predispositions to bring themselves into harmony with it. Radical only in terms of exploring a taboo subject, writers of homoerotic fiction were less inclined to expose sexual activity in detail as part of a generally liberating trend initiated by writers like Henry Miller, James Jones, Norman Mailer, Paul Bowles, etc. than to politicize the homosexual experience. As gay fiction shows, the homosexual, at least until the breakthrough fictions of John Rechy, was less a rebel and adversarial force against a bourgeois society than he was an egalitarian presence crying out for status as a human being who was merely expressing a sexual preference.

Not propelled by strength and breakthrough, the homosexual character in American fiction trends to be a tragic figure and, until the sixties, endlessly, guiltily denying his instincts and seeking to accommodate himself to middle-class social goals, including mainstream sexual orientation. Thus the homoerotic tradition in America has a much more ambivalent but at the same time more romantic engagement with the subject than its international counterparts, say in the self-proclaiming, liberating program of Gide, the rough-trade-upper-class gay love affairs of Isherwood, the jaded nobility of Genet, or the exotic sadomasochism of Mishima. In America the romantic quest for sexual identity, its frequent denial, and the persistent remorse that arises from indulgence in forbidden love limit the forces of rebellion, forcing a love-hate relationship with one's activities, a kind of angst-filled narcissism inhibiting expression and fulfillment through either emotional connection or community. As a result, the American homoerotic novel has remained politically inconsistent, offering in its early phase contradictory impulses to both rebel against the straight world and to forge a comfortable relationship with it and laboring in its revolutionary phase during the sixties to articulate the nature of its politics as if to compensate for its previous deficiencies.

Early writers of homoerotic fiction portrayed the homosexual as a victim of conservative church teachings that prevail in a secular society and take the form of unjust laws militating against the homosexual. Gore Vidal, a spokesman for gay rights early in his career, argued that such laws flouted "the spirit if not the letter of the constitution"[1] and amounted to persecution of a minority group reflecting a whole society's inclination, also expressed in its literature, to distort the reality of the homosexual experience.

While American fiction before the 1940s is not exactly rife with examples of overt homosexual behavior,[2] there were some exceptions, the most notable being *The Young and the Evil* (1933) by Charles Henri Ford and Parker Tyler, a novel depicting the lives of young bohemian gays in Greenwich Village. Others, such as Lew Levenson's *Butterfly Man* (1934), James M. Cain's *Serenade* (1937), Djuna Barnes's *Nightwood* (1937), and Carson McCullers's *Reflections in a Golden Eye* (1941), feature a homosexual or lesbian as the central character. While homosexuality in all of these novels is related to gender confusion and neurosis, a case for Vidal's view might best be made by James T. Farrell's "Just Boys" (1934), a short story that openly engages the theme of homosexual activity as it presumably exists in the underground. Equating homosexuality with violence, perversion, and disease, Farrell attempted to further remove impulses to homosexuality from mainstream society by creating mostly black characters and by restricting the action to the ghetto.

The story is simple enough: Baby Face, a white homosexual, is being treated for venereal disease, which he contracted from a marine he had picked up. Baby Face brings an impoverished black youth named Sammy, with whom he has slept, to a party in Harlem, where he hopes to find Caesar,

Baby Face's former lover, who has left him for Kenneth. Sammy is heterosexual and goes to the party because Baby Face has promised him money. At the party Baby Face is humiliated by the others, and when he reveals the fact of his venereal disease, Sammy, now believing himself to be infected, murders him with a razor.

In "Just Boys" homosexuality is clearly depicted as being depraved and unnatural; most homosexuals in the story are transvestites, and all are effeminate, sexually dissolute drunkards or masochists. They are, in addition, uncontrollably emotional and become flustered by the slightest provocation — they cry and faint, and indeed, as one cop at the murder scene comments, they behave "like a regiment of hysterical old women."[3] Ironically, comic drag queens, homosexuals committed to personal reform, and gay trade with complex sexual orientation would surface in later homoerotic fiction, especially in Burroughs, Selby, and Rechy.

But in the immediate postwar time, some writers seemed to be less on a mission to indicate range and detail of a hidden culture than to destroy the stereotypes by creating melodramatic mainstream fiction featuring characters who were "normal" to the point of blandness and naiveté.

James Barr, author of the early gay novel *Quatrefoil* (1950) and the play *Game of Fools* (1954), accused writers who had previously dealt with the subject of being purveyors of pornography, creating a peep show for an audience that views the subject with "morbid fascination." Barr hoped that someday "the world will see the homosexual for the first time, not as a monstrosity, but as an average human being with the same graceless foibles as everyone else."[4]

This view is consistent with Gore Vidal's motives for writing one of the first American novels devoted exclusively to the developing psyche of the male homosexual, *The City and the Pillar* (1948). Vidal says he "set out to shatter the stereotype by taking as my protagonist a completely ordinary boy of the middle-class and through his eyes observe the various strata of the underworld."[5] Jim Willard, Vidal's middle-class hero, is certainly ordinary enough. More social climber than sexual outlaw, Jim learns little from his many experiences, which take place in settings as diverse as rural Virginia, Beverly Hills, New York City, and New Orleans and span a twenty-year period. Throughout, Willard has many male lovers, but he is only interested in recapturing the past and his first sexual experience with childhood friend, Bob Ford, to whom Jim's thoughts return repeatedly and whom he yearns to encounter once more. Yet, despite all this, Jim

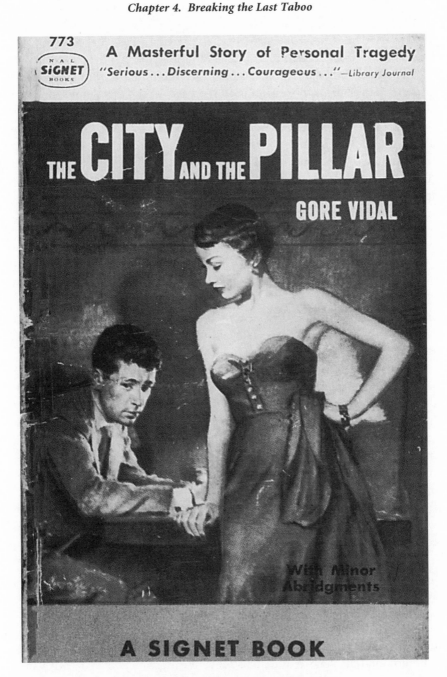

The City and the Pillar, Signet edition, 1950.

steadfastly denies his homosexuality, attributing his sexual activities to harmless diversion or failure to find a suitable female lover.

The title's biblical reference shows the consequence of Jim's illusions and the danger of his obsession with the past. In the first published version of the novel Jim strangles Bob in a hotel room in a final encounter when Bob spurns his advances. In a revised 1965 version Jim rapes Bob after a similar rejection.

In the second version, however, Vidal resisted the temptation to make Jim Willard a more interesting and plausible character. Vidal was still content to shatter the stereotype — that is, to portray a character who is essentially masculine, virile, and athletic (Jim supports himself in Hollywood as a tennis instructor) rather than effeminate and emotionally insecure. Though in both versions Vidal used flashback techniques to show elements of a painful childhood — authoritarian father, Oedipal fixations, etc. — Vidal wanted to show that the primary source of Willard's obsession with Bob is narcissistic worship of the masculine image: "he would study himself in the mirror to see if there was any trace of the woman in his face or manner; and he was always pleased that there was not" (50). Bob is "an ideal brother, a twin" (22), his maleness reflecting Willard's own.

The elitism that would surface in the American homoerotic tradition in the worship of masculinity is somewhat reduced by Jim's repeated denials of his sexuality. Elitism is instead given expression through other homosexual characters in the novel, particularly Jim's older, more worldly lovers. Ronald Shaw and Paul Sullivan are essentially self-pitying masochists who seek out situations that torture them. For Sullivan, cruising bars to find boys to sleep with "gave him the pain he had come to expect and secretly needed." Paradoxically, degradation "sets him apart from others and makes him feel strangely superior to the heterosexual world rather than defensive" if only because "he had a secret that they could not guess and an insight into life that they did not have" (67).

But this is a 1965 perception and one that is curiously absent from the original version of the novel. In fact, Vidal eliminated from the second version any portrayal of the underground at all. And in his first version the underground is represented by posh cocktail parties with New York sophisticates or Hollywood gatherings of entertainment business types, all unsuitable settings for Jim Willard. Jim's simplicity, his fear of being different, and his persistent denials prevent him from conveying with any accuracy the essence of the underground and merely force him to blunder into one disastrous situation after another. Evasion of one's instincts may lead to tragic consequences, but self-delusion and limitation better serve Vidal's polemic of ordinariness than do the compelling and revealing aberrations of his decadent upper-middle-class swingers.

Fritz Peters's *Finestere* (1951) continued the corruption of innocent youth by the misunderstanding society theme that lies at the source of Jim Willard's persistent denial of his true sexuality. Sixteen-year-old Matthew Cameron has a sexual liaison with Michel Garnier, one of his teachers at a French boys' school. The much older Garnier is athletic director of the school, this being consistent with Vidal's profile of masculinity, and again the reader is shown the tragic consequences of forbidden love and its subsequent denial.

The novel devotes much of its exposition to determining Matthew's alienated condition, especially his confused feelings about his parents who he feels have abandoned him — his mother has brought him to France after her divorce to place him in a private school — and his dislike for his new stepfather Paul, a Frenchman who, in a bizarre scene at the end of the novel, turns out to be homosexual and tries to molest Matthew. Matthew's closest friend is Scott, a friend of his parents. Though Scott is not homosexual, he has joined Matthew in France but then falls in love with Francoise, a French girl to whom he gets engaged.

All of this, a rather tedious and long-winded network of connections and estrangements, is ostensibly intended to justify Matthew's despair. The affair with Michel doesn't get started until the second third of the novel when Matthew, in a botched attempt at suicide — he swims too far in the lake and can't make it back to the shore, practically sealing his fate by not crying out for help — is rescued by virile, athletic Michel, and they almost immediately become lovers. This, in fact, occurs on Matthew's awaking; in a scene nearly identical to the climax of D. H. Lawrence's "The Horse Dealer's Daughter," the moment of waking is occasion for rebirth, a resurrection from death and a transfiguration of the spirit: "Something was no longer the same — that moment of death, for it was death, had changed him ... a door inside him had been opened, or perhaps the water had related a spring and had broken through that melancholy dreamlike existence of his, bringing him back to a life that he had never known."[6]

The entire novel, in fact, despite its gay context, has something distinctly Lawrentian about it, certainly in its structure if not in its particulars — specifically, the despairing Lawrence of romantic angst in the early novels. *Finestere*, like *Sons and Lovers*, provides the pattern of the quest for true wholeness as the protagonist tests different approaches to love that are complicated by the suffocating closeness of family relationships and the equally stifling conventional attitudes of society. Matthew's first affair with another schoolboy, Andre, is inconsequential and generates a sense of guilt because there is no love involved. Matthew's relationship with Scott is nonsexual, isolating him further, and it is not until the affair with Michel that all guilt and attempts to rationalize it are finally obliterated:

> There was no question of good or bad, right or wrong, normal or abnormal. It was as useless for him to pretend that a volcano had a right to erupt. He had exploded into life, a process that defied judgment. It was not a question of approval or disapproval, acceptance or rejection; he could not have been more dominated by what he felt if he had lost the power of reason entirely [137].

Michel, too, is delivered from an aimless life of drifting in the Parisian homosexual underworld and from an unsatisfying affair with an Englishman. The older man, however, despite being also changed and revitalized through Matthew's "superior strength," is more skeptical and cautious than Matthew, who Michel believes "was not face to face with reality" (150).

Still, the affair is strengthened, again in Lawrentian fashion, by an idyllic summer on the French coast where the two lovers travel with Matthew's mother and stepfather. It crumbles shortly thereafter when Matthew goes to Paris for a reunion with his father. Unlike many novels of homosexuality, the Oedipal situation is absent here; indeed, Matthew feels no animosity toward his father, and in fact, it is the relationship between his father and Edith, the stepmother whom he meets for the first time, that causes Matthew to have a rather abrupt change of heart as he contrasts their apparently happy and normal relationship with his own hidden and duplicitous one with Michel: "However much Michel might talk about normality, abnormality, right or wrong, the essential wrong was their inability to achieve what he felt from these two people. His instincts told him that such a balance was impossible for himself and Michel" (256).

With rational contemplation restored, Matthew suffers guilt and asserts the usual denial that he is homosexual — "I love you, that's all" (265), he insists to Michel — a desire for reform once he accepts the truth and ultimately suicide after confessing his relationship with Michel to his mother, who violently rejects him. As Lawrence suggests in the uncertain conclusion of "The Horse Dealer's Daughter," the world is a constant and formidable threat to mutual commitment, a condition put at infinitely greater peril in *Finestere* by gay isolation and repudiation by the straight world of family and friends.

It is useful to speak of two types of homoerotic fiction — early works, which depict the tragedy of obsession, fear, self-denial, and self-hatred based on an inability to reconcile the self with an intolerant society, and later works, which attack the uncomprehending prejudices of the larger society. Early fictions were usually conservative, sentimental, and tragic, lamenting their protagonists' inability to express an authentic self. James Baldwin's *Giovanni's Room* (1956) was a transitional novel, showing, like those books that preceded it, the denial at work in homosexual trauma but also showing characters who seek solace by destroying their sensitivity and ultimately pursue ways to feel love and passion less acutely.

Baldwin, in his second novel, recapitulated earlier themes of obsession with the past formulated in the fiction of his predecessors — in Vidal Jim's maniacal desire to recapture it and to reenact it, in Peters Matthew's desire to reconcile it with a more meaningful present. Baldwin's protagonist, David, experiences a desire to reject and to escape the past: "People who remember court madness through pain, the pain of the perpetually recurring death of innocence; people who forget court another kind of madness, the madness of the denial of pain and the hatred of innocence; and the world is mostly divided between madmen who remember and madmen who forget. Heroes are rare."[7]

As the action of the novel demonstrates, David may clearly be identified with madmen who forget. The French setting of *Giovanni's Room*, while revealing an autobiographical dimension, is also a metaphor for the distance that David, an expatriate American, wishes to put between himself and the past, characterized by the familiar Oedipal situation, and especially by David's first homosexual encounter as a teenager with a boy named Joey, whom he quickly rejects.

The pattern of rejection continues throughout the novel. David, clinging to conventional morality, experiences both heterosexual affairs, primarily with his fiancée, Hella, which give him respectability but no satisfaction, and a homosexual liaison with a young Italian, Giovanni, whose love fulfills him but generates guilt and shame, and whom he also

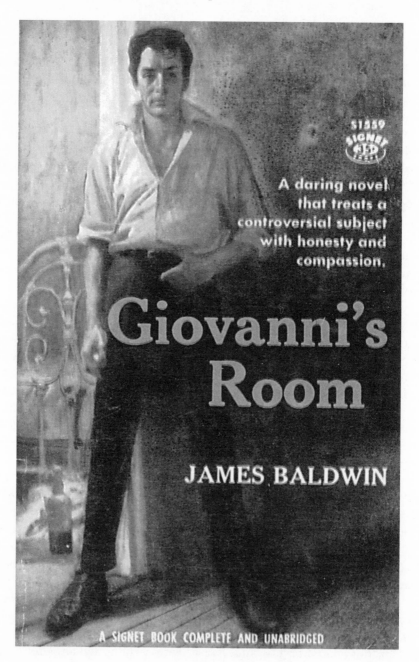

Giovanni's Room, Signet edition, 1957.

rejects in an effort to have a normal love affair with Hella. By virtue of David's heterosexual relations, he is a much more divided character than those in previous novels, torn between a need to fulfill his instincts and the awareness of his chosen denial. Indeed, Jim Willard's sexual awareness is an evolving if labored recognition, its delay resulting not so much from self-conscious rejection as from stubborn idealism, his forced belief that the spontaneity of his first experience constituted a great lost love. Matthew Cameron, on the other hand, rejects his affair after he becomes fully aware of its taboo nature and the repugnance that loved ones demonstrate when they learn of it.

What is common in all of these novels is the discovery and subsequent loss of the true animal self — the maintenance of which is central to the Lawrentian proposition — and in each case the tragic consequences that arise from attempts to tame, deny, refuse, or squelch its reemergence. In *Giovanni's Room*, death again is the result: Giovanni's murder of aging homosexual Guillaume and his subsequent execution.

Despite the atmosphere of repression, the linkage of forbidden sex to dirt, guilt, and fear, *Giovanni's Room* presents in the character of Giovanni one who has fully accepted his sexuality. The romantic novel of homosexuality, overwrought and melodramatic because of its emphasis on love as precondition for passionate fulfillment, prevents the reader from getting a true perception of the homosexual underground, since in these books the underground is generally viewed unfavorably — as a place where mechanical and impersonal sex prevails. In its sentimental portrayal of Giovanni, a guiltless innocent who is ultimately victimized by love, Baldwin's novel is no exception. ·*Giovanni's Room*, however, points to the future direction of the homoerotic novel by giving a better sense of the underground than does earlier fiction, depicting it as a place that provides relief from the unbearable sense of responsibility that homosexual love thrusts on the individual. It is the desire for respite from turmoil that compels David to pursue sailors in the underground after he fails to find fulfillment in heterosexual love with Hella. Reflecting on the intensity of Giovanni's passion after abandoning the Italian, David reaches a reluctant epiphany: "The burden of his salvation seemed to be on me and I could not endure it" (98).

As long as the homoerotic novel attempted to show middle-class heroes resorting to modes of rejection that lead to tragic ends — victims of themselves and a heartless society — the underground remained a peripheral theme. But in the process of countering narrow assumptions about homosexual behavior, another stereotype was being created. Inevitably, it came to be perceived that social adjustment to a mainstream society was not possible and that liberation from oppression and bigotry could only be achieved in the underground. Declaring themselves exiles from the straight world, homosexuals formed their own region, an underground milieu in which community and sympathetic human connection might flourish.

Tennessee Williams's "Two on a Party" (1954) is a short story about two Times Square sex hustlers — a faded, good-hearted female lush and a disillusioned writer on the skids — both bruised victims of a provincial, narrow-minded society who find solace in companionship. Williams's story is as sentimental as most early homosexual fiction, though Williams sounded the note of protest and announced the terms of liberation from an oppressive straight world that would set the tone for more realistic and ultimately less idealistic depictions of gay street life.

> It was a rare sort of moral anarchy, doubtless, that held them together, a really fearful shared hatred of everything that was restricted and which they felt to be false in the society they lived in and against the grain of which they continually operated. They did not dislike what they called "squares," they loathed and despised them, and for the best of reasons. Existence was a never-ending contest with the squares of the world, the squares who have such a virulent rage at everything not in their book. Getting around the squares, evading, defying the phony rules of convention, that was maybe responsible for half the pleasure in their outlaw existence. They were a pair of kids playing cops and robbers, except for that element, the thrill of something lawless, they probably would have gotten bored with cruising.[8]

But the simple romantic rebellion of Williams's characters would be compromised in almost all future homoerotic fictions. The mature works of the genre indeed depicted members of an underground community forging an eternal state of anarchy, but the terms of the conflict were not directed exclusively at those others outside the parameters of the underground. *Queer*, William S. Burroughs's second work of autobiographical fiction, written in the mid-fifties but not published until 1985, was one such novel. Remarkably consistent with later works of homoerotic fiction in its adversarial stance, its absence of accommodation to conventional morality, and its direct treatment of the homosexual subculture, *Queer* particularizes an anarchy, typical in Burroughs, that generates chaos rather than harmony within the underground. As Graham Caveney has noted, though the aim of most gay activists has been "to reappropriate negative stereotypes, Burroughs appears to have taken a perverse delight in perpetuating them."[9]

The protagonist of the novel, set in Mexico City during the forties, is William Lee, a recently recovered morphine addict, who pursues young Eugene Allerton and eventually forms a sexual liaison with him. What little action there is in the novel takes place largely in seedy bars where Lee holds court, delivering long, improvised monologues he calls "routines," in which he performs the fantasy role of Texas oilman, or discourses on subjects like chess, his own homosexuality, or the terrors of thought control. The result of these routines is annoyance and often the complete revulsion of all those around him. Lee's mission to alienate is continued in his other activities — prowling the city with a loaded .22 revolver he occasionally brandishes, drinking heavily, ogling young boys, and taking photographs against their will.

Burroughs has commented on his interest in Mexico City, a place "sinister and gloomy and chaotic, with the special chaos of a dream," one of many decaying cities in his fiction:

> The city appealed to me, the slum areas compared favorably with anything in Asia for sheer filth and poverty, people would shit all over the street, then lie and sleep in it with the flies crawling in and out their mouths. Entrepreneurs, not infrequently lepers, built fires on street corners and cooked up hideous, stinking, nameless masses of food, which they dispensed to passers-by.[10]

The ideal environment for Burroughs is always a primitive and totally corrupt one without restriction and containing the promise of some bizarre fulfillment. Indeed, though Mexico is a place of danger, Lee's greatest fear is not the threat of sudden violence. Burroughs has written, "I live with the constant threat of possession, and a constant need to escape possession, from control."[11] Lee is on an unusual quest — to seek out degradation as a means of exorcising internal evil and to escape external forces that menace him (for Burroughs there is no difference).[12] Lee's public persona reveals a fragmentation of the self, usually a display of masochistic impulses generated from perverse aspirations that he is well aware he is not likely to fulfill.

Lee's pursuit of Allerton is the first of these invitations to self-abasement. Allerton is a drug user, often besieged by junk sickness, and whose condition, as Burroughs has asserted many times, makes him indifferent to sex — for the junkie nothing matters but the next fix. Yet, despite Allerton's indifference and antagonism to Lee, Lee continues to invite the misery of a nonreciprocated love affair. In addition, Allerton has chosen to live without commitment or expectation and is possessed of a rather insipid demeanor, further making him a poor subject for the focus of Lee's affections. Other subjects of Lee's lust, particularly young Mexican boys, are even less promising hosts for consummation, though they inspire wild sexual fantasies in Lee in which he is the center of their attention.

Throughout the novel Lee wills his vicarious postures, and, though masochistic, they become odd forms of assertion, invariably preventing him from projecting any consistent personality. Lee seeks out others to observe him as he acts out various scenarios of degradation. Lee is interested in what he calls "the strategy of random behavior,"[13] and his every action is part of a determination to evade any pattern that might reveal the real Lee. Hard-boiled and elegant by turns, Lee slips effortlessly from a crude to an aristocratic presence, each gesture an escape from the apparent self that preceded it.

But Lee's project of asserting inferiority, it turns out, is actually the inversion of his desire for power. For Lee, "safety lies in exterminating whatever produces the environment in which you cannot live."[14] Routines inspire and promote willed resistance to invasion of consciousness. Not only does a distorted image of the self protect him from violations of the self, but it creates the necessary distance that allows him to better observe life and himself. In the eternal clash of wills, uncertainty lets him form his own patterns of action, to act out and ultimately to violate the self, and sometimes, indeed, the body of the other. Mostly, though, Lee must settle for surrogate violations. Taking pictures of young Indian boys thus represents one form of power: "Many so-called primitives are afraid of cameras. There is in fact something obscene and sinister about photography, a desire to imprison, to incorporate, a sexual intensity of pursuit."[15]

At the end of the book, Lee's search for yage, a special plant that enables telepathy and thought control, is the culmination of his desire to escape and to dominate. "Think of it: thought control. Take anyone apart and rebuilt to your taste. Anything about somebody bugs you, you say, 'Yage.' I want that routine took clear out of his mind."[16]

In *Queer* Burroughs's routines reflect the perceptions of a man reduced and contracted by obsession. *Queer* is a far more fascinating and complex book than *Junkie*, and a transitional work in the Burroughs canon. A legendary book, unpublished for thirty years, *Queer* reveals not so much Burroughs's paranoia of systems of control, the central theme of his later work, as it does revulsion from others. For all its genuinely funny, deadpan humor, *Queer* is a frightening book, presenting Burroughs as a rejector of life, though at the same time the complete man of the underground — isolated, defiant, somehow heroic in establishing a surrogate dream world that actually heightens his sensitivity to his nightmarish existence. Love, such a central theme in Vidal, Peters, and Baldwin, is never part of Burroughs's world because preservation of self is what counts most; the existence of an inviolable self forms the center of Burroughs's universe.

Burroughs's will to power is a consequence of junkie withdrawal — the cure generates an inevitable reintegration with the world that the alienated safety and insulation of the addict's life precludes. As I will show in the next chapter, junk is an unacceptable vehicle to transcendence for many authors because it creates passivity and invites manipulation and ultimately invasion. Yet life without junk, as dramatized by Burroughs, creates a desire to satisfy the ego through sex and other forms of domination (the desire to reduce the threat to the self includes various rituals, not all of them sexual). For Burroughs, writing provided immunity from invasion, but the ego, which he attempted to protect in *Queer*, he soon realized must be shattered to create a new reality, unhampered by fixed notions of the self, a state he attempted to realize by inventing new fictional forms.

But in the narcissism of homosexuality, competition, invasion, and possession, the self is made vulnerable. In the romantic novel of homosexuality there is value in the Lawrentian notion of losing oneself in physical love and passion. This is not the case in those novels in which the underground creates the central context. The antiheroes of Burroughs, Selby, and Rechy want to escape not into love but into an impersonal netherworld, an existence separate from the mainstream and antagonistic to it in every way. Hustling is a metaphor for self-protection, self-projection, and sexual wish-fulfillment, though these too are self-inflating romantic preoccupations.

In *Last Exit to Brooklyn* (1964) by Hubert Selby Jr., the underground is predatory; egos are projected, and an exaggerated sense of the self is proclaimed. The underground in Selby is a primitive country of atavistic

Last Exit to Brooklyn, Grove edition, 1964.

impulses, where love and emotion are scorned and noble feelings have no place. It is the obverse of the early homosexual novel's project to demonstrate the normal through the typical and commonplace — the world of fear, anonymity, exaggerated femininity, the freak show of drag queens. Like Lee, the denizens of the underground create false personae to protect the real self, every gesture elaborately staged to disarm those who act from genuine motives alien to the hustle.

Last Exit typifies homoerotic fiction of the 1960s, both in its sexual candor and in its rejection of love as a motivating force in homosexual activity. Everything in the novel is defined by the deep-seated desire to satisfy need — the cringing need of the outcast to score a fix or to fornicate or to escape the demands of a society that condemns him.

Selby is in Burroughs territory here. Rather than provide pleasure and fulfillment, sex functions in the novel as an invasion of the body, a violation, a means by which someone may gain dominance in the perpetual conflict within the underground. Sex can be humiliation, pain, pleasure, or escape, irrespective of one's desires. Ambivalence is extended to love and hate. Harry Black hates his wife, and his assaultive behavior is intended to give her pain; instead, it gives her pleasure, increasing her devotion to him.

Selby's dark ironies consistently reveal love to be an unwanted emotion that produces weakness and makes one vulnerable to pain. Though Selby's novel mostly concerns transvestites and homosexuals, this applies to heterosexuals as well. After a brief love affair with a soldier on furlough, Tralala, street hustler and prostitute, violently rejects all tender feelings, preferring the isolation of degradation to personal sentiment. She invites a gang rape on herself in which hordes of slum dwellers "tore her clothes to scraps, put out a few cigarettes on her nipples pissed on her jerked off on her jammed a broomstick up her snatch then bored they left her lying amidst the broken bottles rusty cans and rubble of the lot."[17]

Tralala's return to depravity is a disaster, but she nonetheless reenters the unthinking, unfeeling theater of the primary.

In another of the novel's four sections, "Landsend," the nightmare of domestic squalor in a Brooklyn housing project is depicted: shiftless husbands, studs on the make, desperately lonely working mothers, abused wives, etc. Heterosexual love is defined by animal need and momentary gratification, a temporary escape from despair. Hatred and violence characterize domestic life, and there is again no place for human emotion in the brutal milieu.

Other sections of the novel present street hoodlums of unequaled nastiness and the previously unexplored world of transvestites. In "The Queen is Dead" section, Selby projects the politics and elitist tendencies that by the sixties clearly dominated the homoerotic novel. Selby's queens arrive at an inflated notion of themselves by not concealing their homosexuality but in taking

> a pride in being a homosexual by feeling intellectually and ethically superior to those (especially women) who aren't gay (look at all the great artists who were fairies!), and with the wearing of women's panties, lipstick, eye makeup (this including occasionally gold and silver — stardust on the lids), long marceled hair, manicured and polished fingernails, the wearing of women's clothes complete with padded bra, high heels and wig. (15)

The downtown queen pops pills and smokes marijuana and is often persecuted by heterosexual males. Georgette, the central figure, is beaten by her brother and has the misfortune to fall in love with Vinnie, a contemptible street punk who eventually follows Georgette's brother's example.

While homosexuals tend to suffer abuse in Selby's world, they enact a wild revenge in the longest and most interesting section of the novel, "Strike." Harry Black, shop steward of Local 392 and militant union man, is, despite his blustering queer-bashing, a latent homosexual. He is married to a woman to whom he makes love aggressively, without feeling, "with the force of and automation of a machine" (108). Selby turns the proletarian novel upside down in his depiction of Harry, the lumpen proletariat as slob. Harry is a defiant and effective union organizer, fierce in his antagonism to the company during the strike. Yet despite his hardheaded authority, his arrogance extends to the workplace, and Harry is disliked by everyone. He is an incompetent lathe operator who struts around the factory "in defiance of all the rules and regulations" (114). He tells lies about his sexual conquests of women and makes himself obnoxious to his fellow workers by "telling his stories, or a joke about a queer who had his ears pulled off; occasionally sticking his finger in someone's stomach and farting; or asking someone when they were going to buy him a drink" (115). Moreover, he steals money from the union to buy beer for the strike office and, later, gifts and dinners for his drag queen lovers, always to create an image of self-importance.

Harry's aggressive maleness, his bullying of his wife, and especially his reckless behavior during violent strike confrontations with the company give him identity and status in a male world in which conflict is predominant and frequently resolved by physical force; this is contrasted with his clumsiness and vulnerability in the homosexual underworld. If the professional conflicts between himself and the company and the private conflict between himself and women can be easily projected or hidden by macho role-playing, the rite of passage to the subculture is less easily achieved. Harry is unaware that the target of hostility on the part of drag queens is precisely men like Harry, the macho male, who they believe is the very image of admiration for an anti-homosexual American society. Drag queens like Ginger and Regina get revenge on such males by subtly torturing them, and Harry, in his confused inexperience, is powerless against it.

> Ginger put her hands on her hips and watched him lumber towards her, feeling the power she had over him and started dragging him around the floor, stamping heavily on his toes and lifting her knee up into his groin from time to time Harry wincing but still trying to smile and drunkenly trying to get close to her. Ginger pinched his neck fiercely with her fingernails and laughed as Harry's eyes closed then patted him on the cheek and rubbed his head. That's a good dog. Do you know how to beg for a bone, lifting her knee into his crotch ... stepping on his foot and grinding her heel into it ... Ginger flexing her hard muscle, bending her arm and squeezing Harry's hand, wallowing in the joy of holding Harry immobile with the bending of her arm, feeling like David, not killing Goliath with one stone from his sling but slowly twisting him down and down and down with the simple twisting of one massive finger with her small dainty like hand ... the little faggot conquering the giant with the crotch of her arm; his eyes asking why but no question formed in his mind, just instinctively trying to free himself of the pain ... Ginger wanting to yell I'M MORE OF A MAN THAN YOU. (164)

Despite such bullying, Harry imagines fulfillment in the underground when he falls in love with Regina, a queen who eventually abandons him after Harry is no longer able to steal from the union expense account. When Harry is rejected, he becomes self-destructive, seduces a ten-year-old boy on the street, and is subsequently beaten by Joey, Vinnie, and Sal, bloodthirsty neighborhood street punks who break his arms and leave him for dead. Harry's fate is not unlike the tragic resolution of Tralala and Georgette; emotional engagement and the quest for human fulfillment are debilitating, hopeless dreams, antagonistic to survival in the marginal jungle, leading to a crumbling of the self and masochistic wreckage.

In Selby's urban world a struggle for power dominates. This is the case even in the strike itself. Harry is being used by the union as a diversionary pawn, the "built-in patsy" whose function is to reprioritize company strategy: "Harry forced the company to fight so hard, and spend so much time getting what they were allowed under the contract that they didn't have time to infringe on the limitations the contract set on them" (189). Even the myth of union solidarity is made ironic in Selby's vision of a milieu of isolated opportunists perpetuating broken connection and ruthless individualism in the name of unity.

Selby's chaotic and menacing underground is in some ways a forerunner to John Rechy's detailed portrait of a male hustler in *City of Night* (1963) if only because various sections of the book had appeared in little magazines as early as 1957. The Mardi Gras section of Rechy's book had also appeared prior to its publication in *Evergreen Review* no. 6, a fact testifying not only to the antiestablishment nature of the subject matter but also to the nontraditional means of publication sought by underground writers. Taken together, these two books constitute radical statements about gay life in the underground and remain unqualified classics of underground literature.

Like Selby, Rechy was drawn to underground outcasts, and also like Selby, his work attempts to define the depraved, fascinating humanity of his marginal subjects. Rechy's narrative is also as revelatory of the coarse aspects of the underground as Selby's is, though in Rechy the narrator is always in view, interspersing his account of his own participation in the underworld with ruminations about street life and its connections to his past and to his evolving spirit.

For Rechy's unnamed narrator, the underground represents an escape from his unhappy Texas environment, which includes the failure of his classically trained musician father, the narrator's devotion to his mother, and the recognition of his own mortality, the absurdity of a finite existence first pondered during childhood following the death and burial of his pet dog: "There was no soul, the body would rot, and there would be nothing left of Winnie,"[18] observes the narrator. The plunge into the dark world of homosexual hustling is ostensibly a plunge into an engagement

City of Night, Grove Weidenfeld edition, 1988.

with life — a shedding of the spirit that inhibited the Texas boy who "felt miraculously separated from the world outside; separated by the pane, the screen through which nevertheless — uninvolved — I could see that world" (17–18). Sex constitutes a means of momentarily transcending one's own mortality (hence the obsessive fear of aging), and movement is a way of turning valuable moments into something larger, more important — existentially meaningful. Rechy shares Kerouac's sense of the journey and the power of the moment to transcend time and open the self to discovery.

But Kerouac's characteristic enthusiasm is undercut in Rechy by a sense of disgust before a lucid realization of failure. His journey is far from being a plunge into freedom, which might result in self-discovery. The narrator maintains detachment and self-conscious refusal of interaction. The male hustler is safe from commitment only if he has sex for hire and if he maintains an existence away from the underground, say in a hotel, where he can isolate himself whenever he is not hustling. Thus the plunge into life is an artificial one but by necessity generates the illusion of freedom and aloofness signifying that though the hustler gets his sustenance from the underground, he is not part of that world. At best, he is connected only for the moment, then goes on to the next score. As in Selby's world, the underground restricts connection: "After all there's this to consider: the world's no fucking good. You've got to pretend you don't give a damn and swing along with those who really don't — or you go under" (169).

Appearance is important. The male hustler parodies masculinity and maintains artful poses of toughness and manliness just as the drag queen parodies femininity. Pose is everything.

The narrator's motives are complex and revealing. Hustling, for him, betrays a sign of worth — sex for hire without love satisfies the attention that the narrator craves: "And so, in the world of males on the street, it was I who would be desired in those furtive relationships, without desiring back — the money which I got in exchange for sex was a token indication of one-way desire: that I was wanted enough to be paid for, on my own terms" (54).

A combination of narcissism and remoteness, a craving for attention, motivates the narrator's plunge. In addition, for the hustler frantic activity — sex hunting in gay bars, hotel rooms, movie houses, and alleyways — represents a kind of revenge on life's disappointments. The need to dramatize one's existence by promoting youthful vitality through sexual contact is for the narrator preferable to acknowledging an aging body and a flagging spirit.

> Away from the streets, I was wasting my youth. The end of youth is a kind of death. You die slowly in the process of gnawing discovery. You die too in the gigantic awareness that the miraculous passport given to the young can be stripped away by the enemy time ... youth is a struggle against — and, paradoxically, therefore a struggle towards death; a suicide of the soul [237].

The narrator's attempts to crush his innocence, tantamount to disassociating himself from all feelings of pity and compassion, are nonetheless incompatible with his need to separate himself from the underground. His isolation signifies a desire to hold onto his moral individualism, a reluctance to immerse himself completely in petty cruelty and degradation. His initial aloofness stems from this — an inability to steal the wallet from one of his first scores. When he later gets the chance, he does steal it, his theft constituting a breakthrough, a triumph. But the narrator is closest to being transformed into a true denizen of the underground in the presence of Neil, a score who likes to dress up his connections and who claims to be on a mission. "My movement will be an upheaval: nothing is sacred, except violence and power" (265), Neil declares, happy to be the recipient of pain that the narrator administers.

The conflict between the artificiality of the pose and the genuine need to be wanted, albeit in a nonreciprocal way, is exposed in the climax of the novel — a crowded, neon-lit New Orleans at Mardi Gras time, where the costumed decadence of ritual serves to promote the narrator's contemplation of the masks assumed by the hustlers and their various scores. Compelled to reveal truth after watching the various deceptions of several queens revenging themselves on the straight world, the narrator lets his mask slip, confessing to a pair of potential scores,

> "No, I'm not the way I pretend to you — and for others. Like you, like everyone else, I'm scared, cold, cold, terrified."
> Predictably, I became a stranger to them. They had sought someone else in me — the opposite from them, and I had acted out a role for them — as I had acted it out for how many, many others? [341].

This epiphany of sorts is followed by a debate about need and authenticity with Jeremy, a score who elicits further confessions from the narrator. The analysis that the orgasm represents a kind of transcendence into definition, a rebellion against psychic and physical deterioration similar to Mailer's existential revolt, is also seen by the narrator as being part of the masquerade, an inauthentic gesture imprisoning the hustler further in a role, perpetuating the existence of a dream world that conceals a dreaded and lonely isolation. Denial of love is again the reason for the mask. But the narrator, who has put such stock in rebellion, is not about to embrace the liberating value of love, which he fears may itself be an illusion:

> In this room, the world in flaunting before me what could, if tested and found false, be its most deadly myth ... love ... love which, even in the beginning, was revealing itself as partly resignation; perhaps offering only the memory of an attempt to touch ... implying hope of a miracle in a world so sadly devoid of miracles [366].

Assailed by his failure to accept the possibility of love, the narrator contemplates a vision of the apocalypse — New Orleans obliterated in a conflagration of fire and destruction — and sees death as the one true reality. The narrator emerges from this vision free from illusion, especially the illusion of control, distance, and autonomy, and submits to the spectacle of life, the perception of the failure of his journey and an impossible longing to return to his departed innocence.

Rechy's sensitivity to possible violations of the other echoes deep-rooted questions about invasion and violation of the private worlds of the individual pertinent to fiction about the underground. He reveals his misgivings by confessing that "it was difficult to write that book. Guilt recurred as I evoked those haunting lives. Oh, was I betraying that anarchic world by writing about it — or even more deeply so if I kept it to myself those exiled lives?" (xiv).

But in *City of Night* distance itself is an illusion, a pose, and the realization that the narrator is not as remote from the world he describes as he pretends to be is purifying. In reconstructing events from memory, the writer surrenders control and becomes aligned with the subjects of his past, discharging his former illusions of power. Rechy's realignment with the objects of his narrative eschews distance, and the creation of the narrative becomes a gesture of expiation, a way of recovering violation by engaging in purpose, a Wolfean exercise to find order through internalization. Rechy recorded his movements in the narrative, and like Kerouac he was inspired by and reacted to his objects of contemplation.

But it can only be in memory that the narrator unites himself with the sights and sounds of the world he inhabited because his reconciliation with that world can finally never be possible. The writer is able to see the futility of discharging rage and hostility to society in acts of perversion and sadomasochism, the nature of a rebellion that is played out and dramatized through confinement and limitation in the underground. Deception is indeed the eternally operative condition of the underground, a rebellion against retaining fully human identity and determining the terms of one's existence. But it is precisely this fatalism of perception which distinguishes the condition of the narrator, as we see him in the end, from the underground characters that he describes throughout the novel. These others — the professor, who grotesquely regards his homosexual activities as research; Lance O'Hara, who seeks expiation from guilt in love; Neil, who resorts to fantasy by dressing up hustlers as gladiators, pirates, cowboys, motorcyclists, and policemen; Sylvia, who tries to impose rules on the chaos of the gay bar she owns; and the rest — are defeated by illusion, all having less philosophical obsessions and ultimately less political inclinations to rebellion than the narrator. He perceives in his final epiphany the folly of their deceptions:

> The roots of rebellion went far, far beyond the father beyond the mother. Beyond childhood — and even birth.... Something about the inherited unfairness — that nobody's responsible but we're all guilty. Something that has to do with Destiny — and with so many other things: starting out with a legend about a God who cares — and the discovery of a paradise we're all deprived of ... replaced by a prejudiced heaven.... Something about the fact of death, of decay — of swiftly passing youth: the knowledge that we're all sentenced to live out our deaths slowly, as if on a prepared gallows.... And something about the fact that the heart yearns is made to yearn for what the world can't give [357].

Though most novels of homosexuality conclude with a protagonist's recognition of inner defeat, they also conclude with the character's greater awareness of life, an internalized response to the unfair terms of existence or to the cruel, inflexible standards of society. This new awareness is often a hard-won consequence of a search for one's identity and true nature. The satisfying of inner urges requires immersion in an underground milieu that though encouraging solitary pleasure and often conflict, ultimately and painfully prevents denial and false means of protection. Rechy, Selby, and Baldwin especially dramatize the failure of the underground to exempt the self from the responsibility to others. Even though these excursions into the underground drift into nihilism, they do not disguise a basically romantic vision of life that is contrary to the terms in which their protagonists imagine liberation — a vision that exposes truth at all costs and refuses the viability of retreating from human connection.

In his book *The Sexual Outlaw* (1977), Rechy defines the homosexual subculture as the only legitimate form of continuing political revolt against the heterosexual majority: "Since his is a minority defined by its sexual preference, gay energy flows in two areas — the revolution of the sex hunt and the revolution against bigotry."[19] But in attempting to create his own world, the homosexual fails to transcend the pressures of the straight world, which ultimately leads to self-hatred expressed through sado-masochism. Promiscuity, the weapon of the gay revolutionary against the straight world, is acted out in various perverse rituals. At every turn the guilt imposed by the straight world, which the homosexual outlaw never seems to escape, undermines the antinomian energy of his rebellion. The details of the gay underground seen throughout *City of Night* and Rechy's many other books about the homosexual subculture reveal that values of punishment and humiliation are at work not only in the S&M rituals symbolized by leather, handcuffs, police and nazi drag that make fascism fashionable but in the hustler's own rituals of sexual dominance. These rituals of the gay underground demand that the narcissistic hustler imitate the role of oppressor and that the guilt-ridden score become his victim, thus celebrating the straight world's repressive laws rather than transcending them. As David Bergman has acknowledged, in most gay fiction, "the choice is between two limited options: either invisibility or demonology, either objectification as a gargoyle of sexual perversity or obliteration as the ghost of self-abasement."[20]

Still, fiction about homosexuals remained the most political of underground fiction types, preserving the possibility of liberation through self-exposure and insurrection.

The exception is of course Burroughs. For him human connection also invariably inspires self-loathing and impulses to domination, but in his fiction the dream of solidarity is excluded — each man must face the terror alone. His works consistently show the meaninglessness of community, political expression through promiscuity, or radical protest. In fact, Burroughs's works reflect his desire to leave the body behind; they are an attempt to reject physical experience and the material world. But Burroughs is unique among homosexual writers discussed here because he exposes his intriguing duality — exploring the possibility of liberation through both the frenzy of orgy and the passivity of heroin, the latter of which, during his apprenticeship as a writer, promised to be a more amenable solution for a man with his unusual sensibility.

5

Which Way Is Up?
The Drug Novel

The focus on a changing society, and the consequent belief that such change was antagonistic to the existence of an authentic self, inspired searching picaresque narratives in the postwar period. The gay and the Beat novel used the search to reveal responses to social conflict and to achieve an affirmation of the self through decadent beohemianism and uncompromising behavior. With the focus on intensifying personal experience, the subject of drug use was well-suited to this new fiction, which exposed previously unexplored forms of liberation.

But for the drug addict, outer movement was eschewed in favor of an inner journey, an interiorization, a probing of the self celebrating the kind of narcissism that proved unacceptable to many writers of homoerotic fiction. The isolated world of the drug addict constituted a most extreme and defiant resistance to larger pattern making of the culture. Total removal from the mainstream culture, distrust of the other existing within the underground milieu, and essential nihilism, themes central to the drug novel, provide a glimpse of a world that was seemingly alien to the social standards of the larger culture. Ironically, it was a world that was far from immune to invasion by codes central to the mainstream.

In the forties drug addiction was a fresh subject for American fiction,[1] though it had long been a familiar one in European literature as early as the mid–nineteenth century in the works of De Quincey and Baudelaire. As Jean Pierrot has pointed out, drug use as a literary subject had been inspired by a social phenomenon:

> It was during the Franco-Prussian War of 1870 that morphine was first used on a large scale by German, then French, doctors as an anesthetic to alleviate the distress of severe wound cases

or during amputation. The war over, however, these doctors, still unaware of the risks involved, tended to continue prescribing the drug on a permanent basis to patients suffering from nervous disorder. From then on as consequence of such ill-considered prescriptions, the number of addicts throughout Europe was to increase steadily.[2]

Similarly, the increase of drug use in America was linked to the medical use of morphine as a painkiller in World War II. But other parallels, and not merely historical ones, could also be made between foreign and domestic literature about drug use. In France the decadents and their important descendants, the surrealists, saw opium as a means of escape from a tedious and sad world, as well as a way to stimulate new sensations and to tap the unconscious. Drugs as a literary theme appealed to many writers of underground fiction who sensed that the whole culture was moving beyond reason, beyond simple feeling into pure sensation — as if with danger, fear, and chaos pervasive everywhere, only the senses could be trusted. Thus the novel of addiction is populated by dropouts of every sort rather than questers: those who have withdrawn from the search and who prefer confinement and stasis. In junk they find not a temporary refuge in the face of growing materialism and totalitarian systems but rather an alternative way of life that exempts the user from participating in a corrupt social process.

The most radical celebration of junk euphoria in the literature of the postwar period is undoubtedly Alexander Trocchi's *Cain's Book* (1961). As John Arthur Maynard says, for Trocchi, "Whether he was actually shooting up or only writing about it, his absorption was minute and complete.... His awe of the ritual even included a diehard romantic's faith in its higher significance."[3]

But drug fiction, like most other underground fiction, had humbler, more traditional beginnings. Unlike most authors who were themselves homosexuals or drug addicts, and could relate firsthand experience about the social and psychological realities of these subcultures, Nelson Algren, who wrote the first significant American novel about drug addiction, *The Man with the Golden Arm* (1949), was himself not a drug user. Algren, in fact, had little contact with the drug subculture until the mid-forties, when he formed a friendship with a group of junkies.[4] As a result, exposure of the details of the drug underworld was less central to his narrative than it would be in junkie chronicles to come, addiction seen here primarily as one more tragic element in a mosaic of guilt and pain affecting the lives of inner city dwellers.

That Algren sought to celebrate aspects of marginal life other than drugs, however, as well as to chart the dissolution of that way of life, is apparent in his novel. The attempt to sympathize with the dispossessed of the inner city and to capture their speech and show their vitality extends back to Whitman's impulses to celebrate the common man — including the forgotten or left out — and prevails throughout Algren's work. This tradition would continue in Kerouac and Rechy and, especially in the convergence of narrative voice and characters, in Hubert Selby, who displayed Algren's ambivalences at their most extreme. At the same time, the dominant effect of Algren's novel is that of naked, despairing realism reflecting a flawed and paralyzed community beset by betrayal both from a larger system outside of it and by corruptive forces within it. In the late forties, Algren found a debilitating ennui in the underworld that seemed inconsistent with the power and threat of primitive energy seen in the more traditional naturalism that had influenced him — in London's human beasts or in Crane's dangerous street toughs — and, later, in Mailer's and Kesey's urban supermen. In Algren's third novel, adversarial behavior is canceled by withdrawal. His world is shrunken and removed from possibility, its political energies short-circuited by an oppressive society, its inhabitants powerless exiles. In fact, Algren's novel represents a turning away from the Marxist politics that had given authority to his first two novels of social protest, *Somebody in Boots* (1935) and *Never Come Morning* (1942), an abandonment of political idealism and an inquiry into the indignities of urban life. While others after Algren would offer hope for survival in the urban jungle through confrontation and self-assertion, in 1949 Algren was lamenting the disappearance of a genuine American individualism.

The Man with the Golden Arm revolves around the world Algren knew, Chicago's Division Street neighborhood. Its hero is thirty-year-old Frankie "Machine" Majcinek, a professional card dealer whose talent is legendary — "It's all in the wrist 'n I got the touch,"[5] says Frankie. But his boasting barely conceals his truly enervating addiction to morphine, which he has inherited from treatment for a shrapnel wound he received during the war. The origin of Frankie's addiction suggests crushing naturalistic forces at work far beyond the individual's ability to control, but the tragedy is compounded by limited possibility, both circumstantial and temperamental, restricting physical and social movement. An injury to Frankie's wife, Sophie, which she sustained in a car accident that occurred when he was drunk at the wheel and that he believes has left her crippled for life, generates profound guilt. As the novel develops, Algren holds out possibilities for salvation both in the love of Molly Novotny and in Frankie's aspirations to be a professional jazz drummer. But potential for recovery is undermined by the limitations of Frankie, whose prospects narrow after he resumes his morphine habit: "It would be Molly-O or a quarter-grain fix, he'd never make it alone" (131).

Frankie's narrow horizons result in an inclination to withdraw into the self and thus to become further victimized by those for whom any movement at all represents an escape from the dread of place. Given this sense of stagnation, Algren's characters are not unlike Beckett's heroes in a realistic setting, as they consistently acknowledge their narrow plight. Thus even the car accident that injures Sophie and inspires Frankie to marry her is a sort of deliverance from the inertia of their lives: "Something had been made to happen in their lives at last" (77). Moreover, Sparrow, Frankie's devoted friend, speculates on his own ability to get into trouble: "If it wasn't for trouble I'd be dead of the dirty monotony around this crummy neighborhood" (19). Frankie and Sparrow and the rest of the novel's losers are representative of Algren's truly disinherited, who are beyond hope but contribute to their own tragic destinies because they "no longer cared. They were truly unsaved, over the hump from redemption and the hour for turning back lost forever: too late, forever too late. So they hurried forward all the faster into the darkness" (219). Algren's denizens of the underground consequently turn to petty thievery like Sparrow, to prostitution like Molly, or to the pleasures of morphine like Frankie.

But Frankie's escape is a singular kind, not an outward leap, however limited, into lawlessness, but inward into further limitation and passivity. Frankie welcomes all forms of withdrawal in which he is relieved of the responsibility for his life. Even jail provides an "iron sanctuary," giving him respite from burdens he would rather abdicate than control. With Frankie temporarily in jail, we are told, "Frankie Machine wasn't happy; yet Frankie wasn't so sad. He felt oddly relieved now that, for awhile at least, all things could be solved for him" (203).

Junk, like prison, is an isolating, self-absorbing agent that deters self-definition and determines the path of the user's life. Addiction collapses the need for choice and removes goal-seeking in a self-created existence of junk chaos.

Consequently, Frankie's addiction is also a form of self-flagellation, recompense for not having found a place in the world. But if Algren's novel graphically presents details of junk sickness, the self-deluded psychology of the user, the effects of various drugs, clinical descriptions of various cures, preparation of morphine, and other horrors of the junkie life, it also reveals the ecstasy that junk delivers to obliterate the pain of living: "It hit all right. It hit the heart like a runaway locomotive, it hit like a falling wall, Frankie's whole body lifted with that smashing surf, the very heart seemed to lift up — up — up — then rolled over and he slipped into a long warm bath until one orgasmic sigh of relief" (66).

Still, because Frankie's habit reduces him in a world that is crumbling, he is both more aware of the quality of his own suffering and more vulnerable to weakness and defeat than others around him. In many ways Algren's novel is a lament for a world in which human vitality exists but where rich potential is damaged by the encroachment of a bourgeois world that the subculture increasingly resembles. Thus the outcasts of the novel practice exploitation, disloyalty, and duplicity with the same effectiveness as the larger society.

Much of the novel details the friendship between Frankie and Sparrow, who worships Frankie with blind devotion. Nonetheless Frankie "had never fully trusted Sparrow, the punk thought much too fast for him. In this world of petty cheats, small-time children, louts and stooges and glad-hand shakes, one always had to be on guard" (156).

This inability to trust proves a handicap to Frankie in his attempt to make human connection with Molly-O, for despite his desire to "let his guard down" and be "the real Frankie Majcinek" with Molly and to "become what Molly had once glimpsed in him ... what she knew he might be" (245), he cannot be free from his fear of emotional bonding or his skepticism: "He wasn't ready for anyone's trust. He had been too long-trained in wariness to drop his guard that low, that low, and that fast" (298).

While it is true that paranoia is a central theme in the novel of drug addiction, *The Man with the Golden Arm* objectively supports the need for such skeptical defensiveness on Frankie's part. Indeed, Algren's city is besieged by the spirit of dread, competition, and isolation. Sophie observes that "familiar doorways had come to look menacing in the morning light, ready to be slammed in the face of anyone who knocked at all. Nobody was home to anyone else anymore" (106). And Frankie's distrust of Sparrow is justified: Sparrow runs out on Frankie and lets him go to jail for stealing electric irons. Moreover, Sparrow is instrumental in getting Frankie hunted down for the murder of the pusher Louie Fomorowski.

The latter, the result of a ploy from the police to trap Frankie, suggests the two elements that most limit the mobility of the disinherited: exploitation and guilt. The losers are exploited by agents from within the subculture, dope pushers such as Louie who raise the price of a fix, and from outside by Record Head Bednar, the police lieutenant who pits one against the other in an effort to solve Louie's murder. Bednar personifies the oppressive society that condemns and limits the dispossessed. What is large and impersonal and generally unseen in Beat and homosexual fiction is given definition in the drug novel and in much fiction of the sixties, especially in Mailer and Kesey, that dramatizes explicit subcultural opposition to systems of oppression. The guilt characterizing the doomed outsider is, however, shared by the police lieutenant. Recognizing that "there were no men innocent of intent to transgress ... if they were human, look out," he nonetheless feels that he has betrayed those who "had all along been members of himself—theirs had been the common humanity, the common weakness and the common failure which was all that now could offer fresh hope to his heart" (316–317).

Despite Algren's attack on the source of institutional persecution of the disinherited, such strategy results in only a minor compensation: the law machine is relentless, the net descending on Frankie for the murder of Louie, despite Molly-O's efforts to hide him from the police.

What remains is Algren's hostility to the society that forces characters like Frankie to withdraw into a self-nullification that precludes rebellion. The despair found in Algren at this point in his career represents a protest of cosmic proportions aimed at the very terms of existence that had first made him abandon Marxism and eventually even the writing of novels until he could find a more suitable form or purpose for writing them. In his next novel, *A Walk on the Wild Side* (1956), Algren abandoned the drug metaphor and employed techniques of the comic picaresque. Borrowing from Henry Miller and anticipating Kerouac, Algren celebrated in his novel the rogue's quest to embrace larger spaces of America. Ambivalent, as Kerouac was, to the elements of cool that would emerge in various Beat narratives embodied not only in the hipster but in the addict, Algren could see no way out in bleak withdrawal, but in his one novel about drug addiction he created an appropriate metaphor in the drug

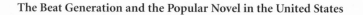

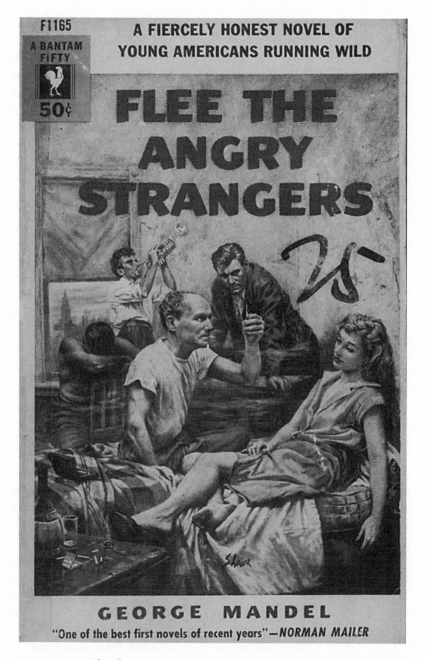

Flee the Angry Strangers, Bantam edition, 1953.

experience for the stifling, fractured, claustrophobic, dead-end existence of Frankie Machine's West Division Street, Chicago.

George Mandel's *Flee the Angry Strangers* (1952) recapitulates some of Algren's themes — particularly the sense of confinement and the taking of hard drugs as an alternative to emotional connection and moral commitment. However, recognizable forces such as guilt and institutional exploitation are not in evidence as instruments of repression. The historical moment, a transition between Algren's view of hopelessness and a freedom to choose dissolution, is captured here. The underground characters of Greenwich Village are affected by a profound inertia generated by meaninglessness that can only be dispelled by desperate indulgence in the new, albeit internalized experience, because conventional alternatives (job, family, etc.) constitute ways of living that are simply too wretched to contemplate.

In contrast to Frankie Machine, Diane Lattimer, the eighteen-year-old protagonist of the novel, is representative of the young and impressionable who gravitate to the Greenwich Village underworld of Bleecker and MacDougal Streets. Diane reflects Mandel's attempt to represent the self-destructive tendencies of the new youth culture generally, contrary to Algren's portrait of an isolated junkie ruined beyond his years and who inevitably gives in to the decline that accompanies spiritual defeat. Diane, despite being a recent mother, resists the influence of her own mother, whose Christian values and respectability compel her further to embrace bohemian self-indulgence: "Mama wanted her to go to God, but she'd go to the ungodly. There were not many roads for the trapped: climb a tower to heaven or drown out your brain; you can't long endure reality!"[6]

Diane's defiance does little to suggest that her world is less narrow than Frankie's. Her story is also the story of the Village others who seek in drugs and sex the vehicles to create a self-contained world of aimless pleasure: "They hustle by day and ball by night, or hustle through darkness and sleep past the hours of the sun, but they never brought the outside in, neither newspaper nor magazine nor tale of anybody's woe. And days went by uncounted with everyone in his private habit" (165).

And even though the attraction to the Village constitutes an attempt to realize an existence outside of the conformist mainstream, no community exists there; nihilism is the shared perception and withdrawal is the only virtue. Mandel's characters lack the vitality of Algren's, whose creator celebrates their speech and the thriving life of an underworld where, despite ennui, there still exists a certain purity and style, a doomed but wondrous reality. And though junk is pervasive in the Village as one form of alternative activity, it is not sought for purposes of spiritual transcendence. Nor do Mandel's young desperadoes bear much resemblance to Brossard's sophisticated swingers or to Holmes's intellectual seekers. Mandel's characters are doomed, decidedly unhip, with no value system to counter their alienation. The Beat novel represented a search for new values and the means to transcend spiritual dislocation through drugs, visions, movement, sex, community, and jazz. Bebop was the new music of the mid-1940s, and it challenged the rigid rhythms of swing by emphasizing spontaneity and rhythmic innovation. To the Beats bop was more than simply new music. It was the soundtrack for a new, energetic lifestyle invoking individual expression, freedom, and new consciousness. But bebop is dismissed by Mandel's characters, not recognized as an element in the formulation of a new aesthetic. And Diane, the hedonist nonartist, is not tentative in her rejection of modern jazz: "It's supposed to be new jazz. Supposed to, but it isn't happy like jazz or sad like jazz can be. It's just — I don't know — it's like the horrors, like sick or something" (75).

The absence of strong personalities exemplifying a quest, or characters who possess Nietzschean values like Henry Porter, Dean Moriarty, or McMurphy, further reduces energy and direction. Characters like Dincher, Lukey, and Joe Letrigo are superficial pessimists, escapists "bored with day-to-day living which had been chasing them into one situation after another" (77). They are typical urban victims, though less self-conscious about their disengagement from a larger world than Algren's dispossessed or Brossard's and Holmes's Beat bohemians.

Only Robert Stoney, a veteran of the Village scene, has potential to function as a character with initiative directed externally rather than internally. But Stoney, despite his eloquence, waxing philosophical about the predicament or humankind and the Village's place in the wasteland, is treated contemptuously by everyone. Generally acknowledged to be a pompous windbag, a tiresome fixture in the Village, Stoney ultimately reveals himself to be more opportunist than prophet, changing identity as often as he shaves off his beard. Stoney runs the gamut of roles from impoverished artist to lover of Diane's rich and respectable mother.

Moreover, Stoney's sermons of cultural doom are simply not welcomed by the denizens of this underground. The Village, Stoney says, is "the world in diminution. It's all the ineptitude, the waste and vapidity

106

crammed together for imaginative purposes. Man's inadequacy in a nut-shell, ready to be examined" (34). Actually, this observation characterizes the culture Stoney analyzes accurately enough. But for young people who cannot accept the divisive mendacity and compromises of their parents — and who engage a cult of failure — detachment, silence, and escape are preferable to embracing galvanic forces found in art, conversation, and historical speculation.

The Beats were in search of the other who could model a politics of salvation or perhaps assume a leadership role to reduce suffering in the urban wasteland. But Mandel's characters willingly participate in the corrosive scene, wallowing in ennui, without hope, like passive juvenile delinquents who have lost their cultural bearings. Even talking, in those marathon rap sessions central to the Beat ethos, offers no solace to the emptiness of living: "It seemed talking had been a substitute for living this night, that it was a carnival of the despairing, all of whom had uttered their formula for conduct and in talking had succeeded only in sounding lame excuses for the turgid totals of their days" (228).

The single character in the novel not given to pompous sermonizing or nihilistic withdrawal is Carter Webb, Diane's brother-in-law, whom she loves. Carter represents a kind of sympathetic moderation to the others' all-out irresponsibility, but he is fully antagonistic to the bourgeois world. Carter works as a film processor and often serves as arbiter between Diane and her mother during their frequent battles, which usually end with Diane's mother threatening to commit her daughter and with Carter encouraging emotional engagement and human connection as a solution to their conflicts. But even Carter is vulnerable to spiritual displacement, excess, and dissolution as a participant in the life of the Village subculture, and he must struggle against full identification with the others.

> Long nights in the unbroken wail of a thousand sourceless voices, he had looked through that violet-tinged light, over tables packed with dope fiends and philosophers, prostitutes and poets, artists and hoods, darling dreamers, derelicts, and every American variety of displaced person, all together in a debris of Babel which some conciliatory side of him had defined as fundamental human affinity never seemed fundamental enough. (21)

Drifting toward despair, Carter is a provocative example of the new confusion, and his belief that positive action may result in salvation ironically leads to his tragedy. Though he acts as the conscience of the Village disaffiliated, whose withdrawal disqualifies them from caring, Carter lacks a full perception of the dangers of the drug underworld. Buster, the impotent drug dealer who vows to kill Diane, ultimately murders Carter by throwing him through a window when Carter tries to protect Diane from him. Those who care too much and harbor illusions of order in the underground do not survive it.

But Carter nevertheless fulfills Mandel's role as observer of the Greenwich Village subculture and provides a mouthpiece for the author, who peers over the edge to lament the self-destructiveness of the young while at the same time being critical of the dead-end moralities of an older generation. Mandel's novel accurately captures the confusion of the moment, the drift, the optionless self-indulgence of middle-class characters who reach into the abyss by choice. Junk, treated less clinically and revealingly in this novel than in either Algren or its chief chronicler and spokesman, William S. Burroughs, symbolizes a substitute world of frighteningly narrow proportions in which curiosity, quest for meaning, and faith in transcendence are trumped by a desensitized chaos in which the characters are content to lose themselves. Mandel's novel suggests that even understanding and charitable action may not penetrate the wills and psyches of the lost who wish to stay that way. At one point, as Diane reaches the nadir of her ambitionless existence, she perceives Carter as "a man who knew where he wanted to go and why, too presumptuous an attitude for her" (438).

William Lee, the first-person protagonist of William Burroughs's first novel *Junky* (1953), is something of a departure from Mandel's numbed drifters desperately seeking states of oblivion. Though Lee, like Mandel's young junkies, enters a drug underworld to escape the boredom of middle-class existence in a Midwest suburb where "all contact with life was shut out,"[25] he is constantly on the move, active in the underground as street hustler in New York, junkie in New Orleans, and homosexual alcoholic in Mexico. Yet neither is Lee on a typical Beat quest for fulfillment; rather, his movements always originate from a need to escape his present circumstances. Whether he travels from New York to New Orleans when he feels the law closing in, or from New Orleans to Mexico when he can no longer trust his drug connections and clients and has to take the cure, Lee is set on immediate change but not psychic or spiritual evolution.

Unlike Mandel, Burroughs asserts the value of his days as an addict; he is skeptical about both the community of losers that Algren presents

with such compassion and about the virtue of being a moderate sympa-
thizer like Mandel:

> I have learned a great deal from using junk: I have seen life
> measured out of eyedroppers of morphine solution. I experi-
> enced the agonizing deprivation of junk sickness, and the plea-
> sure of relief when junk thirsty cells drank from the needle.
> Perhaps all pleasure is relief. I have learned the cellular stoicism
> that junk teaches the user, I have seen a cell of sick junkies silent
> and immobile in separate misery. They know the pointlessness
> of complaining or moving. They know that basically no one
> can help anyone else. There is no key, no secret someone else
> has that he can give you. I have learned the junk equation. Junk
> is not, like alcohol or weed, a means to increased enjoyment of
> life. Junk is not a kick. It is a way of life [xvi].

The desire to lead the junkie life as an authentic alternative to a bourgeois existence is recounted in the prologue to the novel: Burroughs's
neurotic, nightmare-filled childhood; his sheltered, empty youth; his early
reading with tastes generally running to European decadents like Baudelaire and Oscar Wilde; his fascination with criminality; later, his hatred
for Harvard, from which he graduated; his choosing occupations such as
private detective, bartender, and exterminator that would involve him
with low-life characters; and, finally, his addiction to narcotics, which he
used because he "did not have strong motivations in any other direction"
(xv).

On the contrary, Burroughs himself, and not as William Lee, had
strong inclinations toward criminal exploitation that began with minor
unprofitable illegal stunts like breaking and entering or shooting chick-
ens in the country with a .22 rifle or driving his car recklessly. He later
consummated his interest in genuine criminal activity, which is largely the
focus of this novel's confessional drama, by making his way through the
underworld as a lush-worker (a specialist in robbing drunks on the subway), securing morphine through phony prescriptions, and finally by
pushing heroin and getting addicted. As for serious brushes with the law,
Burroughs was arrested for possession in New York in 1944; for drunken
driving and public indecency in Texas in 1947; for illegal firearms in
Louisiana in 1949; and, in his most famous escapade, for the shooting of
his wife, Joan, in Mexico City in 1951.

Clearly, Burroughs was not content to be a mere romantic eavesdropper on crime to suit a rather esoteric Beat-like program to violate laws of a bland society; in Burroughs's consorting with criminal outcasts, rather, the details of which were well collected in his early autobiographical novels, we see his desire to live at the center of violence, even thrusting himself into situations that lead to it. Inspired by his immersion in the criminal life and by heroin addiction, which prompted a direct and terrifying vision of the underground, Burroughs depicts the junkies of his fiction as dehumanized individuals, driven and defined by the intensity of their need. Joe the Mex, Louie the Bellhop, George the Greek, Eric the Fag, and the notorious Bill Gains are malicious, lifeless, predatory creatures given to crime and betrayal.

Thus, Algren's fractured community is given a further look in Burroughs's matter-of-fact, virtually clinical recounting of the world of drugs and addicts, a grim hierarchy of parasites and opportunists. Burroughs saw more clearly the struggle for power both inside and outside the underground when he later wrote *Naked Lunch* (1959), a novel in which the line between legitimate commercial activity and criminal activity is blurred. But the process of convergence that leads to mutual exploitation and antagonism in both arenas, and ultimately in resemblance of the subculture to the mainstream, can be glimpsed in his earliest work. His books suggest that institutional efforts were made to control the trafficking and consumption of drugs, a course that was symptomatic of generally oppressive forces in the society at large. Because of its documentary nature, *Junky* goes further than *The Man with the Golden Arm* in objectifying oppressive systems and in showing the breakdown of subcultural variance. Hospitals where Lee goes to take the cure turn out to be oppressive totalitarian bureaucracies. Later, the police constitute the onerous antagonist, adopting fascistic methods of surveillance and detection, stopping addicts on the street to check for needle marks and, if discovering any, trying to get the addict to sign a statement admitting to his condition, thus making it a crime to be an addict. Outraged by this development, Burroughs declares, "This is police state legislation penalizing a state of being — other states were emulating Louisiana. I saw my chance of escaping conviction dwindle daily as the anti-junk feeling mounted to a paranoid obsession, like anti-semitism under the Nazis" (79).

The implications and consequences were naturally grist for paranoia.[7] At the end of the novel Burroughs's junkies no longer resemble the zoot-suited downtown hipsters who speak the hip language, a coded jargon presumably protecting them from surveillance. As the underground eroded due to strong-arm tactics by the police, subcultural distinctions disappeared. Infiltration was so great that not even one's witnessing a junkie taking a shot in the arm would relieve suspicion that he might actually be a federal agent trying to snare another user. In fact, Lee suspects that addict-agents were being recruited into the police force for just that purpose. Finally, Lee disdains the new generation of users who are reminiscent of Mandel's weary escapists because they lack "energy and spontaneous enjoyment of life" and after taking a fix "slump into a chair like a resigned baby waiting for life to bring the bottle again."[8]

Outsiders in general constitute a threat to the self-absorbing isolation of the junkie life — a voluntary alienation from conventional aspiration and morality or, in Robert Creeley's terms, "an alternative logic to organized 'goodness' or 'purpose.'"[9] But Burroughs's narrative does little to obscure parallels between the day-to-day efforts of the junkie to obtain illegal drugs and those of the middle-class consumer to obtain legal consumer goods. As in all underground fiction, the junkie life, though constituting a headstrong form of social dissent, illustrates the impossibility of liberating oneself from the fundamental patterns of the larger society. John Arthur Maynard notes that the junkie life has profound affinities with the life of the mainstream citizen in its reliance on the consumer ethic: "If junk were anything, it was a consumer product. The difference was that unlike cars, expensive scotch, ranch-style homes, and all the other commodities commonly sold with the promise of heaven and earth, heroin actually delivered."[10] Perhaps for Burroughs a redemption of sorts could be found in the knowledge that "if the junkie debased himself more than the ordinary citizen to obtain the product he needed, he also had fewer illusions about why he needed it."[11]

By the time he wrote *Naked Lunch*, however, Burroughs no longer privileged one form of addiction over another; for him, all sources of addiction, legal and illegal, constituted menacing agents of control. During the 1970s Burroughs's metaphors prevailed in the American drug novel. In Michael McClure's *The Adept* (1973) and Robert Stone's *Dog Soldiers* (1974), competition for illegal substance control is a barometer of the corrupt and disintegrating state to which America has fallen. These books depict the exploits not of the passive user but of the dealer who willingly and knowingly participates in an unwholesome contest with the enemies around him to regain the coveted power source. Heroin in these novels becomes the impetus for engagement in a world bereft of value in which greed, conflict, and inevitable violence become the prime urges.

Critics have acknowledged the link between *Junky* and Burroughs's masterpiece *Naked Lunch*, particularly in terms of the oddball characters, the nightmarish urban settings, and the moments during junk sickness of hallucination — horrific visions of giant insects and the sudden metamorphoses common in both works. However, despite the linear form of his early work, in *Junky* Burroughs was already writing a fractured narrative, his minimalist portraits of hoodlums and a general mood of anxiety signaling an arrested development and structural truncation that cannot be explained solely by his gestures to the hard-boiled realism of Hammett and the requisite need to maintain a quick pace. *Junky* is a nervous narrative, the dominant voice of Lee shuffling off to new subjects as rapidly as possible, as if the narrator distrusts the formal mechanisms of his narrative. Both the awareness of the limits of realism and straight reportage and of Burroughs's paranoiac sensibility were preconditions for the inhibited forms of his early work, but they would also anticipate formal and thematic directions determining the innovative excursions of his later books.

The threat to the underground culture, which Burroughs feared would result in its total usurpation by the control system, made his alienation from humanity complete, and after his failed quest for yage he withdrew completely into addiction. *Naked Lunch* was written in Tangiers during the mid-fifties in a small room in the Native Quarter, where Burroughs injected heroin, recorded his fantasies on notes he scattered about the place, and, according to Burroughs, spent much time contemplating his foot. Burroughs's prolonged state of junk disintegration turned his fantasies into a metaphor for humanity victimized by addiction to power, money, and sex. The routines, celebrated and made literal in his novel *Queer*, in Lee's tactical impositions and inducements to gain the attention of others, become, in *Naked Lunch*, scattered, undifferentiated voices announcing the violence of a world dominated by technology and psychic invasion.

The setting of *Naked Lunch* is Interzone, a symbol of the modern city characterized by rivalry and oppression, and where the battle for psychic control takes place among various parties. Representing the various forms of control are the Liquefactionists, who practice every form of perversion and who believe in the merging of all into one by physical absorption; the Divisionists, who duplicate themselves through parasitic possession and

Naked Lunch, Castle edition, Grove Press ©1959.

who seek to control the proliferation of undesirables ("Every replica but your own is eventually an undesirable"[12]); and the Senders, who seek to control "physical movement, mental processes, emotional reactions and apparent sensory impressions by means of bioelectric signals injected into the nervous system of the subject" or who "render the subject susceptible by drugs" (167).

Overseeing many of the fascistic activities practiced by the parties of Interzone, the police, and the antagonistic bureaucracies is Dr. Benway, archmanipulator and genius of thought control, who understands the capacity of drugs to dehumanize the individual and cause him to regress to a lower form of life. He is a coordinator of Symbol System, "an expert in all phases of interrogation, brainwashing, and thought control" (21). Contact between the victim and his enemy is prevented by an intricate bureaucracy, contact with nature is prevented — all flowers and trees have been destroyed — police are allowed access to every room in the city, and citizens are subjected to humiliating searches. Moreover, they are conditioned by exposure to pain, by threat of torture, and by the pleasure of drugs. "Drugs remain an essential tool of the interrogator in his assault on the subject's identity" (21). The effectiveness of Benway's methods is occasionally revealed, as for example in the Carl Peters episode in which an innocent Every man is summoned to the locus of bureaucratic activity and subjected to sexual humiliation and hypnotic control.

The opposition is represented by the Factualist Party, which presumably cherishes individual freedom in its fight against these various agencies of control. The battle between forces of resistance and forces of control is enacted in violent confrontations in which the city is assaulted by disease, gangs of hoodlums, and giant insects symbolizing the metamorphosis humans suffer when invasion occurs. Only through anarchy may the bureaucracy, which Burroughs compares to a virus, be defeated, for a virus

> can only exhibit living qualities in a host, by using the life of another, the renunciation of life itself, a falling towards inorganic inflexible machines; towards dead matter.
> Bureaucracies die when the structure of the state collapses. They are as helpless and unfit for independent existence as a displaced tapeworm or a virus that has killed the host [134].

Anarchists of the Factualist Party like A. J., the notorious merchant of sex, and Lee, an addict who is taking the cure, and other inhabitants of

Interzone, attempt many strategies to assault the opposition and to elude control. A. J., for instance, scandalizes the respectable facade of Interzone with practical jokes: accompanied by his purple-assed baboon, he pounds a silver stake into the floor of a respectable restaurant; he spikes the punch at a Fourth of July reception at the U.S. embassy with Hashish, yage, and yohimbine to cause an orgy; he puts piranha in Lady Sutton Smith's swimming pool; and he releases exotic bugs at the Metropolitan Opera. Lee, on the other hand, resorts to more violent means of retaliation, gunning down two policemen who come to arrest him. Clem and Jody, members of Islam, Inc., sell defective parachutes to the Ecuadorian Air Force.

Burroughs's wildly funny characters are derived from popular fiction models and function similarly to pop fiction characters as part of some scheme or counterscheme against manipulation and control, which makes his work essentially parodic. The conspiracies overwhelming Interzone are familiar, reminiscent of hard-boiled detective fiction in which city and police corruption dominate; or horror fiction in which alien forces invade to take over the human organism; or pulp science fiction in which a mad scientist discovers ways to obliterate humanity.

But if intimidating forces in popular fiction are countered by lone forces that render such menace impotent or obsolete through the determination of the hard-boiled detective, the virtues of future man, or the resourcefulness of the secret agent, Burroughs provides no heroes to counter Interzone activity because all characters are subject to invasion, all touched by the presiding metaphor that in *Naked Lunch* Burroughs calls the Algebra of Need. Sex and junk, so pervasive in Selby's urban community of the dispossessed, are used in Burroughs as tactics of control. Sex, drugs, religion, and politics are all ways for totalitarian regimes to achieve power and domination over the inhabitants of his universe. The Factualists, the chief members of which are Clem and Jody, are themselves commercial agents addicted to money and power, whose motives for opposing oppression are no more idealistic than to simply boost the value of their holdings. The motives and alliances of A. J. are not known, and the objectives of Islam, Inc. are obscure. A. J. may well be a Liquefactionist agent, since it is impossible to be sure of anyone because "all agents defect and all resisters sell out..." (205). And though Lee, the source of the novel's fantastic visions, is a recovering addict, he is nonetheless subject to a continuing need, since addicts are never really cured. In the book's introduction Burroughs asserts, "A dope fiend is a man in total need of dope.

115

Beyond a certain frequency need knows absolutely no limit or control. In the words of total need: Wouldn't you? Yes you would. You would lie, cheat, inform on your friends, steal, do anything to satisfy total need" (vii).

The subculture in *Naked Lunch*, in constant conflict with both itself and its adversaries, can be characterized as a world in which total instability reigns and every motive and action is an extension of the prevailing chaos. As Eric Mottram has said, "Burroughs has no prophet secreted within his wasteland mythology: sacrificial power of all kinds is the target of his secular vision."[13]

Burroughs, beginning with *Naked Lunch*, illuminated and attacked manipulative systems of control by employing modern techniques to breach language systems, to escape orthodox forms of communication, and to penetrate the unconscious. This aspect of Burroughs sets him outside the company of most writers discussed in this study. Burroughs, like Nabokov, Borges, and Beckett, is part of the postmodern project against the realistic novel and traditional literature's focus on the other; his is a solipsistic project, an attempt to metaphorize the world from observations of himself, whose authority is put into question by an aggressive culture bent on control. Burroughs, as a consequence of addiction, and as a response to a subculture that became pervasively reductive as Gestapo-like powers imposed on sources of difference, turned away from the agents of inspiration that underground writers most often sought to engage. Kerouac and others relied on a personal form of narrative, constructed from past events, celebrating the liberating potential of community, acknowledging the validity of human interaction, and preserving the possibility that connections can be made. On the other hand, what Alfred Chester has said about another important underground writer, Jean Genet, may be applied with equal measure to Burroughs: "He tells us that only in his detachment can he know who he is, can he achieve unity and identity. He is in detachment from all roles and circumstances. His substance is in that which will not enter form."[14]

Burroughs turned away from the other, which led to a completely self-generated narrative in *Naked Lunch*, the fantasies of one man, a celebration of the individual, which precluded salvation through community.

Yet Burroughs undoubtedly recognized the problems and limitations of his narrator, who, if not self-consciously controlling his novelistic materials, has presented elaborate recreations of his own drug experiences through random juxtaposition of voices via collage. Even at the outset of his writing career, Burroughs was concerned with limiting the authority of the artist-narrator to avoid duplicating in art the obsessions with control that he describes so powerfully in his fiction. In his journals he explains the process of distancing he employed in *Junky*:

> I include the author, Lee, in the novel, and by doing so separate myself from him so that he becomes another character, central to be sure, occupying a special position, but not myself at all. This could go on in an endless serial arrangement, but I would always be the observer and not the participant by the very act of writing about a figure who represents myself.[15]

To remove the possibility of imposing patterns of meaning on his fiction, Burroughs invented the cut-up method of composition, the main purpose of which was to limit the authority of the central consciousness that shapes the fiction. *The Soft Machine* (1961), *The Ticket That Exploded* (1962), and *Nova Express* (1964) all contain examples of a technique that combines and rearranges Burroughs's own narrative with randomly selected textual material from the works of other authors. In telling his stories of cosmic instability, Burroughs used the cut-up method as a way to achieve the spontaneity that he believed more controlled methods of composition deny, to renew the power of language that he believed had "lost meaning through years of repetition," and to perpetuate the surreal spirit of Rimbaud's "systematic derangement of the senses"[16] to achieve new vitality. Yet, perhaps inevitably, Burroughs's experiments with randomness and accident were still perceived by him as being analogous to military strategies, methods of protection against psychic invasion: "If your strategy is at some point determined ... by random factors your opponent will gain no advantage from knowing your strategy since he cannot predict the move."[17]

Despite all this, Burroughs's work was not inconsistent with the Beat project with which he is generally associated. His works reflect the spirit of the Beats who sought to expose and break down control systems by directing an attack on falsehood, deception, and enervating pattern-making of the main culture. Yet Burroughs's works also anticipate the dissolution of the Beat ethos. He played out their concerns to extremes and recognized that shared values provide no immunity from infiltration and self-destruction, his vision of the subculture being one of ultimate disintegration. Thus Burroughs, the rebellious visionary, captured the rage of the Beats and other underground subcultures, but he broke from the romanticism that often characterized them. His dark works are reflections of an America whose inhabitants have little opportunity to redeem themselves through communal identity, personal response to nature, individuality, or in spiritual fulfillment through sex. Burroughs's works nullify the latter because, despite the frequency of sex, mostly homosexual, in his books he rejects the physical world totally.

It can of course be argued, as I have done, that the subtexts of most Beat fiction, as well as fiction influenced by it, also dramatize the failure of any adversarial program to liberate the self. But because Burroughs's work is postmodern, questioning the efficacy of signification, valuable more as pure idea than as a revolutionary program of salvation, exposition of the horror is enough — chaos is preferred to stability. Madness and murder as forms of liberation function perfectly well as fantastic allegories but not as practices in the real world. Burroughs is thus the eminence grise of what came to be known in America as metafiction. As Robin Lyndenberg has said, "His aim is to reverse and explode the kind of assumptions about truth, empiricism, and moral norms which form the basis of literary humanism."[18]

During the 1980s Burroughs's career was revitalized by the production of several new novels — *Cities of the Red Night* (1981), *The Place of Dead Roads* (1984), and *The Western Lands* (1987) — and by his cult hero status with the New Wave generation of punk rockers. Though Burroughs's literary accomplices of the forties and fifties like Ginsberg, Kerouac, and Kesey were often identified with the milder and idealistic aspects of the so-called Woodstock Nation, Burroughs's literary experiments and attitudes clearly endeared him to the punk subculture of the seventies and eighties, which aimed its wrath at earlier idealists, defining its lifestyle in opposition to hippie modes of dress and behavior. Ronald Sukenick has perceptively contrasted the New Wave culture with earlier subterranean cultures, and in pronouncing its difference he indirectly revealed Burroughs's special appeal for them:

> What was important for people in Punk and New Wave was image. For previous subterraneans, image was incidental to vision or change in the society itself. While for these newer movements image was an end in itself. Insofar as the inner life was conceived, it was important only in order to exorcise it

through a kind of ritualized psychodrama, whether in slam
dancing or performance art. Image is safe because it is disem-
bodied — you get around better as an image than you can as a
self. It allows you flexibility and ironic distance, and it allows
you to reject an idea without taking its alternative seriously
either.[19]

Likewise, Burroughs, with strategies of indeterminacy and enclosure,
mocks all solutions his underground colleagues relentlessly idealized. In
Burroughs all dreams of salvation are countered with nightmares.

The fiction of Burroughs has true relation to the world he knew, but
so candid was his report from the underground, so extreme his response
to it, that survival rather than growth became its central motif. But other
writers — not only those who wrote about drug addiction — were similarly
diagnosing the excesses of the subculture, which seemed bent on moving
toward chaos. Yet not all of these writers shared Burroughs's skepticism
about idealism and his distrust of the other; in fact, some represented the
very spirit of activism that became more pronounced as the counterculture developed.

6

Capturing the New:
The New Journalism

In some ways the New Journalism of the sixties was a response to the gap left by writers who wrote intensely subjective experimental fiction, like Burroughs, or who made use of fable and myth to create new fictional forms, like Barth and Hawkes. Tom Wolfe, New Journalism's major practitioner and spokesman, believed that experimental writers had abandoned the novel of manners, morals, and society of which underground literature was a part: "I think people are selling themselves short when they want to make the form do the work.... The fact that there might be something new in content or new in comment, is not anything that impresses people once they get into this frame of mind that the avant-garde is on the frontiers sheerly of form.[1]

Though Wolfe shared the general perception of experimental prose writers that new forms were required to meet the demands of an uncertain and shifting reality whose events became progressively more bizarre as the decade went on, he proposed a compromise between objective and subjective views of reality. For Wolfe it was essential for writers to preserve allegiance to a faithful rendering of external reality at the same time as they sought to discover the inner lives of the subjects they wrote about.

> The best thing is to have both — to have both someone who will bring you a bigger and more exciting chunk of the outside world plus a unique sensibility, or rather a unique fantasy life, even, to use the way Freud explains it, a unique emotional reality of his own that somehow echoes or vibrates with the emotional states of the reader. So that you get both the external reality and the subjective reality.[2]

What was needed, Wolfe argued, was to supplement journalism with the fictional techniques generally associated with traditional realism, such as scene-by-scene construction, dialogue, detailed points of view, and what Wolfe termed "detailing of status life"—that is, the recording of everyday gestures, habits, manners, customs, etc., "symbolic of the subject's position in the world."[3] This device in particular was suited to the New Journalists, who sought to capture subcultural activity and marginal life and politically relevant material, all of which were attractive subjects to explore, since they were mostly hidden by the media and underrepresented in the sudden wave of experimental fiction.

Wolfe thus embraced the devices of Balzac and Dickens, incorporating them into his journalism to better represent "what really happened"[4] and rejected the need to invent radically different forms to interpret new reality. Rather than saying that realistic forms were dead, as many experimental novelists were then arguing, Wolfe recontextualized conventional realistic devices, believing that they were still viable techniques that had not been improved on as means to capture and present states of consciousness, though Wolfe's awareness of and willingness to use modernist experiments like stream-of-consciousness gave him stylistic flexibility.

According to Wolfe, tendencies of the reporter to fictionalize, a typical criticism leveled at the New Journalist, were held in check by faithful, on-the-spot research by the journalist, whose task it was to "get inside someone else's world and stay there for awhile."[5] This obligation to observe and to penetrate the scene, to know it thoroughly, to trust personal testimony above everything, and to document changes in the social fabric by peering into unexplored areas of society gave the New Journalism kinship with most postwar underground fiction.

While not exactly acknowledging a tradition, Wolfe did admit to certain predecessors of the New Journalism: Dickens's *Sketches by Boz* and Mayhew's *London Labour and the London Poor*, both books about the lower classes of London; Mark Twain's *Innocents Abroad*, which includes scene and dialogue; Chekhov's *A Journey to Sakhalin*, an exposee of ugly conditions in a Russian penal colony; Stephen Crane's Bowery journalism; John Reed's *Ten Days That Shook the World*; George Orwell's *Down and Out in Paris and London*; the reportage of *The New Masses*; John Hersey's *Hiroshima*; and, in more recent times, *The New Yorker* and *True Magazine*.[6] But whether or not New Journalism had a specific tradition, publications like *The Village Voice, Esquire, New York Magazine*, and *Rolling*

Stone Magazine were quickly receptive to it, and writers like Wolfe, Truman Capote, Norman Mailer, Joan Didion, Gay Talese, and others became vigorous practitioners as well as producers of book-length works in the movement. Of course, the disparities among these writers were numerous. Wolfe tended to be the boldest experimentalist in form, shifting rapidly in and out of characters' psyches with a dexterity and capriciousness rarely attempted by the others.

But all New Journalism reflected a constantly shifting view of reality; perception itself became its subject. Implicit in it was the struggle to interpret events as they happened around the author-investigator, a participant in radically charged situations, requiring risk and discovery that the observer also struggled to record faithfully. The subjectivity that characterized confessional underground narratives now came to be cherished by journalists as well. And the challenge to the old and the traditional by those who favored the new and the immediate widened the gap between young, ambitious writers of nonfiction and the journalistic establishment. Morris Dickstein has noted that

> in this atmosphere of social confrontation and self confrontation the New Journalism arrived to do battle with the bugbears of journalistic convention — with impersonality, with boredom (or "snoredom," as Tom Wolfe calls it), with the insider mentality that kept the reporter dependent on his sources and virtually a fixture in the institution he covered, with an ethical neutrality that turned hostile or exploitative whenever the new culture of the sixties came in for attention.[7]

Hunter S. Thompson's *Hell's Angels: A Strange and Terrible Saga of the Outlaw Motorcycle Gang* (1966) is a model work of the New Journalism. More conservative in his use of formal innovation than Wolfe, maintaining a modicum of distance and even occasionally employing straight journalistic techniques, Thompson is nevertheless thoroughly engaged in his mission to yield the truth, his authority presumably verified by his presence in the work. Moreover, the outlaw biker was a perfect New Journalism subject. He was uniquely American and a genuine postwar phenomenon.

Thompson shows that the cultivation of an image and the implicit dangers in riding are essential to the Hell's Angel's mystique. The author is sympathetic to the romantic definition of the lone, defiant outlaw and contemptuous of the passive, vicarious observer for whom the Hell's Angels "are acting out the daydreams" and "who don't wear any defiant insignias and who don't know how to be outlaws."[8]

Aware of his own role as observer, Thompson the journalist needed to verify his own authority as well as his contempt for the passive and the bourgeois by showing his own recklessness and participation in the unfolding events as often as possible. Thus the author makes frequent reference to his drinking with the angels, as well as to his securing their confidence by taking advantage of his civilian status, as for example his getting by the police to go on a beer run at the Bass Lake gathering. In the closing chapter he even admits to getting nearly stomped to death by several of the Angels.

Thompson shows that he understands the biker mystique from the inside, since he rides a motorcycle himself and knows the exhilaration and danger firsthand, often heading down the dark Pacific Coast Highway at midnight, at great speeds. He compares the thrill to the quickened sensations of the LSD high: "they are both a means to an end, to the place of definition." He wants to experience

> A few seconds on the Edge ... The Edge ... there is no honest way to explain it because the only people who really know where it is are the ones who have gone over. The other — the living — are those who pushed the control as far as they felt they could handle it, and then pulled back, or slowed down, or did whatever they had to when it came time to choose between now and later [345].

The reference to "The Edge," of affirming life at the extreme, persists throughout underground writing, as does the ambiguity it generates in those who are drawn to it yet who must survive to tell about it. The author thus bears an inchoate relationship to the strange breed about whom he writes, sharing some of their values — love of speed, motorcycles, contempt for police and the establishment — yet ever remaining the outsider. Thompson's rancor for the establishment grew legendary in his more outrageous but less satisfying Gonzo journalism of a few years later — yet here, to his credit, as in the most convincing underground writing, Thompson held back to observe with discretion. The truth is preserved by the intrusive reporter, who bears witness to and yet is touched by the crazed self-indulgence all around him.

This schism cultivated by the author allows him flexibility in his report, particularly in matters regarding the Hell's Angels' cultivation of their image, thus creating a hybrid of traditional journalism's objectivity (long sections detailing the origins of the biker menace) and New Journalism's subjectivity.

There is large purpose in Thompson's predilections to objective research. Thompson attributes the Angels' initial infamy to a *Newsweek* account of a gang raid on Porterville, California, and contrasts police reports with what he regards as tentative, unreliable eye-witness versions of the same event. The image of the Hell's Angels as dirty, violent outlaws was, says Thompson, "virtually created by *Time, Newsweek*, and the *New York Times*" (51). Thompson's thesis — that the bikers' cultivation of this myth of despicable toughness was generated by "emotionally biased journalism" (52), which led the Angels to subsequently literalize the image — is supported by his assertion that the biker outlaw phenomenon had no precedent before World War II. In fact, prior to the Hell's Angels achieving national prominence as media subjects, the most notable example of motorcycle gangs engaged in destructive behavior was the Hollister, California, riot of 1947, in which hundreds of bikers ran amok, inspiring the 1951 *Harper's* magazine story "Cyclist's Raid" by Frank Rooney, which in turn became the basis for the Marlon Brando film *The Wild One*.

Thompson claims that the Hell's Angels' mythology created by the media compelled the bikers to enhance the myth "to become even dirtier" (65), and he is explicit about this, maintaining that they would actually urinate on their clothing or dip them in oil to achieve the desired result. Not only do they seek to be as dirty, ugly, and offensive as possible, but they eschew leathers and crash helmets worn for safety by most bikers in favor of the more stylized sleeveless denim jackets, headbands, and peaked Prussian helmets, and they wear tattoos with swastikas, daggers, skulls, etc., intended to encourage their outlaw image.

Thompson's purpose was partly to demythologize the Hell's Angels, to show that while they could indeed be violent, the myth of violence was exaggerated, inflated by an old-fashioned press out of touch with reality, aided by public hostility, self-interest inspiring media manipulation by the Angels themselves, and by general fear among law-abiding people.

Primarily the myth that Thompson attempted to debunk was that of uniqueness; he asserts that the Hell's Angels are actually unworthy of all the attention:

The sloppy histrionics and inane conversation can be interesting for a few hours, but beyond the initial strangeness, their everyday scene is as tedious and depressing as a costume ball for demented children. There is something pathetic about a bunch of men gathering every night to the same bar, taking themselves very seriously in their ratty uniforms, with nothing to look forward to but the chance of a fight or a round of head jobs from some drunken charwoman [119].

Despite their image as outsiders contemptuous of everything civilized, Thompson meant to show that the Hell's Angels are "not so different from the rest of us as they sometimes seem. They are only more obvious" (100). He thus details their roots — white trash sons of Okies, Arkies, and Hillbillies who drifted west and eventually settled in California. Thompson also emphasizes the club's similarities to other organizations such as fraternities, particularly in their reliance on ritual and hierarchy and intense loyalty codes, though their criminal traditions certainly give them profound distinction. And Thompson gives pause to those in that particular moment of the mid-sixties who may have claimed a certain distinction regarding the antics of the Hell's Angels, most notably the very real battles they engaged with the repressive enemy establishment.

The chronic friction between the outlaws and the police, Thompson warns, made the Angels dangerously appealing to some segments of American society, particularly to the bohemian counterculture, which had long expressed indignation on behalf of social outcasts and so naturally romanticized the rebel bikers. The Hell's Angels were of course fashionable for a time in such circles and often mingled at parties with the intelligentsia from Berkeley who, as Thompson points out, wanted to talk about revolt and alienation while the Angels lusted after their women and swilled their liquor. The last section of Thompson's book especially is an attempt to show the misguided attempts by hippie intellectuals to make the outlaws into symbolic heroes, a role to which the Hell's Angels were profoundly unsuited.

The outlaws were always uncomfortable around the hippie drug scene, and even Ken Kesey proved to be an incompatible host; the Hell's Angels' drugs of preference were marijuana, barbiturates, and of course plenty of beer. They never took to LSD because "they were too ignorant to know what to expect and too wild to care" (312) — in other words, they were too low-class to appreciate the subtle pleasures and consciousness-expanding bias of a milieu less basic than their own.

They also sided politically with conservatives, supporting the Vietnam War and attacking antiwar demonstrators in the name of patriotism at the Oakland-Berkeley border. Those who had seen the Hell's Angels as kindred spirits had failed to recognize the seriousness of the bikers' fascist, anticommunist right wing stance, and Thompson regards the attack on demonstrators as crucial in obliterating the mystery and myth of the Hell's Angels. "Overexposure had reduced the menace to an all-too-common denominator, and as the group portrait became more understandable it also became less appealing" (324). It was clear that the Angels had closer affinities with the police than they did with the counterculture, not only by virtue of their working-class background but by a natural predisposition to thuggishness. "They made a place for themselves in the final preserve of male dominance, the world of guns and fists where only lawmen and outlaws were permitted."[9]

Yet while Thompson's presence as active participant and observer in the various misadventures of the Hell's Angels provided him with insight into their activities, his book nevertheless oversimplifies the nature of their menace. Characterizing the bikers more as antisocial revelers than as resolute criminals, Thompson saw the type of violence generated by the Hell's Angels as likely to be explosive, unplanned, mostly affecting those who don't understand the special quality of the hoodlum threat, which Thompson takes pains to define. For Thompson, the Angels are disqualified from getting involved in big-time criminal activity because of their conspicuous image ("the Angels are too obvious for serious drug traffic") and because of their hedonism ("a taste for pot is not part of the formula for success in a profit-oriented society"[10]). Of course to criticize an over-eager press and a dishonest journalistic establishment from which a maverick like Thompson was willingly estranged forced him to undermine the threat of the outlaws by trivializing their power — overstated in the mainstream press — though an additional purpose was to warn sympathizers that the bikers, mere brutes to be avoided, not mythical aliens, had been on the side of the political establishment all along.

In point of historical fact, however, by the early seventies the Hell's Angels were indeed involved in major drug trafficking and practically controlled the California amphetamine market. This activity shattered a temporary detente with the Oakland Police, resulting in a major investigation that led to the Angels making mob-style hits on their own members, competitive drug dealers, police investigators, and unfriendly witnesses.[11]

Thompson's failure to recognize and project the depth of the Angels' menace was generated by a literary approach — an attack on a particular method of journalism. *Newsweek*, the *New York Times*, and *Time*, Thompson claims, were taken in by the Hell's Angels' myth, or saw only what they chose to see. According to Thompson, their myopic, misinformed, and misleading accounts of the Angels overstated the case because conventional reporters had not engaged in proper modes of investigation. Thompson's book, an attempt to set the record straight, was intended as a testament as much to the methods and processes of the New Journalism, which he employed to locate the truth, as to the truth itself. *Hell's Angels* is indeed one of the more interesting products of the New Journalism to appear, but its problems reflect many of the shortcomings of other works in the style — strict allegiance to a countercultural audience and a hostility to establishment thinking that resulted in posturing that inhibited a complete analysis of the material on which it focused.

Thompson's insistence that the Hell's Angels were not sufficiently threatening, moreover, belied a concern that they posed a danger to misled or unaware members of the counterculture who romanticized them. Still, the difficulty of making judgments beyond the confusion of the moment gives Thompson's journalism integrity based on an appropriately styled flow of information and attitude that best illuminated an unfolding phenomenon.

Tom Wolfe, on the other hand, in *The Electric Kool-Aid Acid Test* (1968), seems content to provide a seemingly arbitrary rush of information to tell the adventures of Ken Kesey's Merry Pranksters. Wolfe's project was in part prompted by his idea that Kesey's group was actually a new religious movement in the making. Wolfe stated this in an interview:

> One learns that every modern religion from Hinduism to Buddhism and Christianity to the present, started with a primary group, a small circle of disciples, as they're called in Christianity, who have an overwhelming experience that is psychological, not neurological — a feeling, an overwhelming ecstasy that they have come to interpret in a religious way and that they want to enable the rest of the world to have so it can understand the truth and the mystery that has been discovered.
> The Pranksters were no exception.[12]

Wolfe's approach was thus to celebrate the rituals and process of development throughout; Wolfe, the complete observer, narrates what he sees,

Farrar, Strauss and Giroux, 1968.

rarely interacting with the Pranksters, and is seemingly unchanged by his association with them. Unlike Thompson, the struggle to observe, assimilate, and assess within a properly distanced context, is nonexistent. Nor is the difficulty of communicating with those whom he observes to gain their trust and to better grasp the essence of the situation, a feature of Thompson's practice, even contemplated. Rather, Wolfe sets out as a recording device, a floating camera eye, and with his mixed bag of stylistic tricks, he flamboyantly moves in and out of the Pranksters' psyches. Wolfe's strategy is seemingly a suspended objectivity intended to capture the Pranksters' lifestyle as he practices the holy language of hip, the technique embracing an animated reflection of the moment, the magical and all-important Now. Like the novelist of manners whom Wolfe emulates, the author lets his characters speak directly to the reader, providing a seemingly accurate picture of the human relations he observes.

Superficially, Wolfe's book is an equivalent of the Pranksters' attempt to film the bus trip, replete with a privileged view of the psychedelic experience (necessarily internalized in stream-of-consciousness sections, though not from Wolfe's own experience), incidents at La Honda, Kesey's hippie headquarters, and the Pranksters' activities there, such as acid trips, experiments with audiovisual equipment, game playing, Kesey's rap lectures, etc. The film of the Pranksters made by Kesey was, however, formless, without direction or control. Wolfe's book, on the other hand, is quite controlled, much like Kesey's own literary work — suggesting formlessness but given direction by the subtle hand of the narrator, a formidable presence somewhat smugly secure behind a virtuosic literary style that belies messages about letting go.

Despite some pretensions, however, *The Electric Kool-Aid Acid Test* is a valuable and comprehensive document of the activities of the Merry Pranksters and of the events that precipitated the group's formation. Kesey's eminence as a West Coast catalyst of countercultural practices (acid rock, light shows, psychedelic posters, mixed media entertainment, etc.) — all of which became recognizable components of the underground culture of the '60s in America — is given thorough attention. Wolfe chronicles Kesey's Okie roots, his days at Stanford in the Bohemian quarter of Perry Lane where chemical drug experiments were conducted in 1958 and where Kesey even then gained prominence, the day-glo bus trip with Neal Cassady driving in the spring of 1964, the Trips Festival and Acid Tests, the drug bust and Kesey's fugitive days in Mexico and his eventual capture, all of which pre-dated Wolfe's first meeting with Kesey, and finally Kesey's rejection of psychedelic drugs.

Wolfe's book also reveals that Kesey, somewhat like Kerouac, was out of step with the culture he had helped to create. As Kesey's program of mind expansion evolved from parties and informal gatherings to planned public events in San Francisco's Fillmore Auditorium and Winterland and the counterculture gained recognition, Kesey's own evolution from hero to figurehead, and eventually to myth, shifted. For some late-sixties exponents of an expanded counterculture, Kesey was a figure of unclear motives, obviously at odds with the values of an increasingly more commercial and politicized scene. A perception of Kesey as being too powerful and a potentially destructive force led San Francisco entrepreneurs and media people like Bill Graham and Ralph Gleason to distrust and ultimately to abandon him. Kesey's purpose, if not explicitly religious, ultimately involved finding individual solutions to the antagonisms of a materialistic society, which had initially inspired him to exercise various forms of leadership. Kesey's attempt to distance himself from what he regarded as the less pure or dishonorable aspects of the acid culture, a distancing that led him to try somehow to "get beyond acid," was seen as a power move in itself — a calculated and subversive threat to wreck the psychedelic movement. Wolfe offers a perceptive analogy here.

> It's a little like the socialist movement in New York after World War II — the Revolution is imminent, as we all know, and agree, and yet Christ, everybody and his brother has a manifesto, the Lovestonites, the Dubinsky Socialists, the CPUSA (bolshevik), the Wobblies, everybody has his own typewriter and mimeograph machines and they're all cranking away like mad and fuming over each other's mistranslations of the Message. Not that the heads in Haight Ashbury are wrangling with each other yet, but what do they do about Kesey? Just sit back and let him and the Pranksters do their thing? Let them try to turn a lot of impressionable kids off LSD, the way the newspapers say he intends? Or let him suddenly make a big power play at Winterland and take over the whole movement? Politics, in a word.[13]

Kesey proved to be incompatible with commercial agents, whose aspirations applied in greater measure to personal, financial, or community goals than to individual self-expression and awareness. Kesey's tendency to distrust those with tangible goals who wanted to harness impulses to chaos into social formula is at work here. Wolfe's book ends with Kesey's conviction on drug charges, his incarceration on a work farm, and ulti-mately his defection from the psychedelic movement in San Francisco to an isolated rural life in Oregon.

Kesey was out of the picture, but his tendencies to self-dramatization and guru-like gestures toward liberation through power were tested in extreme measure by another figure relevant to the California countercul-ture, Charles Manson. *The Family* (1971) by Ed Sanders sets out to explain "how a group of young Americans became welded together into a war-like clan that killed."[14] His theories on why the family turned from flowers to knives, hatred, and murder are basically as follows: bitterness gener-ated by unnecessary marijuana busts and constant police harassment and the specter of the equally unnecessary Vietnam War; the will to change to go even further out, reflecting "Manson's need to maintain true magnet-ism" (73); Manson's association with Bobby Beausoleil, veteran of the Cal-ifornia devil worship cult scene, a figure nearly as terrifying as Manson himself; Manson's familiarity with "sleazo inputs," techniques derived from Manson's own study in prison of magic, hypnotism, astral projec-tion, scientology, and subliminal motivation, etc., the purpose of which was to control others; and of course Manson's having grown up into a life of crime. Major attention is given to Manson's early life as pimp, petty criminal, jailbird, and hustler to emphasize his talent as a manipulative, self-aggrandizing mysogonist.

Sanders had long been a member of the counterculture and had pros-elytized its value as poet, rock musician, and free-speech advocate, and he makes his allegiance to the benign elements of the hip underground clear throughout his book, reacting to some of the family's diabolical activities by directly addressing his readers with ironic asides like "shudder, shud-der" or "sound like fun?" (197). But this commentary on the family's bizarre behavior is unnecessary in a book that chronicles increasingly repugnant acts that clearly speak for themselves. Sanders's presence in the text as commentator on the grim events and his liberal use of dialogue dur-ing recreations of the Tate and LaBianca murders are devices borrowed from the New Journalism. But in his ironic concentration on aberration rather than on pattern, Sanders evades his responsibility as analyst of the culture that produced Manson. Sanders, unlike Wolfe, does not abdicate point of view by becoming assimilated into the activities he reports; nev-ertheless, he avoids addressing the implication that bohemianism, in its hatred of the bourgeois life, may be a breeding ground for outbursts of fascism from its own ranks, especially as its political tendencies became manifest.[15] Indeed, a reactionary tendency characterized most workings of the New Left during this period, as was revealed in the violent attitudes and often right-wing, antiliberal rhetoric of the Weathermen and the Black Panthers.

It is the horrendous fact of Charles Manson that gives pause when one reflects on Norman Mailer's prophetic statement in "The White Negro" of the possible consequences of hipsterism:

> It is possible, since the hipster lives with his hatred, that many of them are material for an elite of storm troopers ready to follow the first truly magnetic leader whose view of mass murder is phrased in language which reaches their emotions.[16]

As Mailer recognized, the underground milieu is radical, potentially fascistic, and seductive, possessing destructive qualities that the Beat ethos glimpsed but often downplayed until such territory began to be exposed in other underground narratives of the 1960s. It is in Manson that antinomian, neo-Nietzschean impulses thrive, that antimaterialism is enlarged, and that contempt for the establishment takes on profound meaning.

But Sanders, in his zeal to portray Manson as a cheap, opportunistic hoodlum whose megalomania soared until mass murder was formulated as a goal, often mocks Manson's marginal existence as hustler, which, paradoxically, in another context might have given him cultural authority:

> Around July 22, 1955, Charles Manson drove a stolen 1951 Mercury from Bridgeport, Ohio to Los Angeles, bringing with him his seventeen-year old pregnant wife Rosalie.... He had been in prison since he was sixteen and in various corrective institutions before that since he was thirteen.[17]

This passage, which would not have been out of place in a book like *On the Road*, is here meant to provide the sordid early facts of Manson's life, presumably to explain why he was led to later acts of depravity that Sanders fears have destroyed the counterculture. And Sanders might well be defensive, for it is in Manson that the destructiveness associated with the underground ethos, often buried beneath its idealism and glamour, finally arrives in extremis.

Sanders is correct in asserting that Manson's mayhem reflected a "need to go further" (37), but he sees this more as a need for Manson to maintain personal control than he does as a reflection of the ideal to test the boundaries. Sanders's tendencies to celebrate and sentimentalize the underground serve as denials of the underground's proclivities toward aggressiveness and violence. He describes Kesey and the Pranksters, for example, as benevolent forerunners who were "essentially good" (43), emphasizing the Pranksters' positive activities in contrast to the family's negative ones. Yet the precedent here is indeed Kesey-inspired activity: the day-glo bus painted black by Manson; the experiments with LSD; the filming of group activities; the endless pseudonyms of both the Pranksters and the family; and most important, the emergence of the Christ figure who achieved the total submission of his followers. Sanders attacks that which Wolfe, in Kesey's case, failed to consider:

> Even though he told everyone to do their own thing, to be themselves, his own personal magnetism, combined with a constant process of selection, attracted those who thirsted for a leader. Control was what Charles was into all along, in spite of the claims of liberation and freedom. (38)

Manson is the culmination of the new man that runs through all underground fiction but is given most accurate expression in numerous Beat works — reflected in the search for the heroic outsider in Brossard's hero worship of the heel hero, eventually romanticized by Kerouac and Mailer, and given further momentum by Kesey as the subcultural explosion took shape, supported by gestures toward anarchy and liberation in the proliferation of taboo subjects. Manson is indeed less an inversion of the underground hero than a variation of the theme reflected by the destination sign at the front of Kesey's bus — "further" — its fatal and unfortunate extension. Sanders, in his desperate gestures to preserve the counterculture, attempted to separate the hip from the impressionable — the truly inspired disciple of hip consciousness from the acid zombie. Underground writing began, of course, as a project to distinguish the hip from the bourgeois. But, as the counterculture expanded, writers like Thompson and Sanders became increasingly concerned with different questions about authenticity relating specifically to matters of inclusion and exclusion. Both books are in essence attempts to exorcise reactionary elements from the counterculture.

The Family is also a companion piece to Wolfe's *Acid Test* because it relates a similar quest to achieve mystic transcendence through audacious activities that become more and more questionable. Sanders's book, like Wolfe's, is short on analysis, but it is most revealing as a horrifying portrait of a debased culture thriving on adventure. A larger scene is explored, especially the world of devil-worship cults; estranged and wandering children breaking from a dead middle-class existence; a world of the decadent rich devoted to materialism, drugs, and sex; the dangerous world of the underground dope scene; and a burned-out and vengeful hippie culture. It was the crossover of countercultural values into mainstream life that set the stage for Manson's revolt, including the sudden openness and willingness of the rich to embrace the perverse and the outrageous.[18] Indeed, this was the direct cause of Manson's ability to obtain connections in the movie and music business, to infiltrate the homes of the famous, and to refine a truly impressive talent to achieve influence and notoriety. On the verge of a recording career and with a film deal about the family in the works, Manson was encouraged in his ambitions by elements of the entertainment establishment, a world grown vulnerable by impulses to commercialize what was off-center or in the spirit of radical expression. There was and always will be money in strangeness.

The phenomenon of Charles Manson, his career a grim mockery of the American success dream, represented a fascinating reversal of priorities: the marginal man infiltrating the lives of the privileged on his own terms, entering a civilization gone corrupt, temporarily finding acceptance there, then seeking vengeance and escaping to the wilderness. Manson's revolution was conceived nonpolitically, of course, but it was conceived by using subversive modes of power, the sources of which in Kerouac and Kesey were connected to liberation. The countercultural model used as weapon, its morality long evaporated, was, in addition to a system of liberation, an instrument to break down defenses erected by a privileged culture to distance itself from the downtrodden and to violate it. It was a rebellion that naturalists and liberal reformers could not have envisioned — the smooth-talking hustler manipulating a privileged environment, his intrusion made possible by the mainstream culture's willingness to embrace that which was different.

It was at the same time, of course, an old-fashioned assault on the leisure class by an underling, and it was this precisely that caused real danger to the counterculture. In the aftermath of the Tate-LaBianca murders it meant a further polarization, creating a renewed and intensified mistrust and aversion to the other, a return to oblivion of an underground that had become visible and had begun to assert viable modes of power. It also meant the souring of the ideal that had contained the seeds of violence all along but that in its mass-movement stage had opted for standards of docile community. The Kent State massacre and the violence at Altamont were further incidents that unraveled the ideal and spelled dissolution for open ethics and set the stage for the cultural conservatism of the '70s and '80s.

The political realities of countercultural crisis were best explored by an author who had always held an uneasy alliance with the youth culture. Norman Mailer's *The Armies of the Night* (1968) remains the one masterpiece of New Journalism. In the face of sixties chaos, it alone captured countercultural process at a moment when the counterculture seemed destined to climax either in highly public obliteration or in mass triumph. That neither outcome actually came to pass at the time of the Pentagon march does not tarnish the book's power in retrospect, however. Indeed, Mailer is extraordinarily adept here at identifying and gauging the strengths and weaknesses of the various groups that tenuously meshed to form the countercultural movement during its most politically radical time. Moreover, the book's achievement, its aesthetic success, was specifically indebted to the techniques and strategies of the New Journalism.

If the reticence of New Journalists to abandon ideological bias often led to flawed projects, *The Armies of the Night* was strengthened by Mailer's refusal to identify with any elements of the largely inchoate counterculture. Like Thompson, Mailer savored the acuity of perception that the artist has and that becomes enlarged by his participation in an event charged with mystery and potential violence. However, Thompson's drug-tinged sensibilities, as well as his role as spokesman for the counterculture in the pages of publications like *Rolling Stone*, made it difficult for him to remove himself from alliance with the underground. Mailer, on the other hand, takes pains to distance himself from elements of the counterculture. At the same time he realized that the stoic invisibility practiced by a writer like Tom Wolfe would hardly be appropriate either. According to Mailer, "an eyewitness who is a participant but not a vested partisan is required, further he must be not only involved, but ambiguous in his own proportions, a comic hero ... to recapture the precise feel of the ambiguity of the event and its monumental disproportions."[19]

Mailer thus insists on his alienation from the liberals — "much too nice and principled for him" (81)—whom he means to antagonize by his drunken, laced-with-obscenities speech at the rally the night before the march. Nor is he comfortable with the hippies, to whom he devotes numerous pages of description, focusing on their dress, drug-taking, tribal rituals, etc.—capturing the "status life" of a generation. For Mailer, the American young were victims of postwar brainwashing and were now reeking havoc on the technological, educational, and political evils that had corrupted them. And though he criticizes this postwar generation, primarily because he is dubious about the taking of drugs, Mailer is fascinated by the existential nature of its revolt: "It had no respect whatever for the unassailable logic of the next step: belief was reserved for the revelatory mystery of the happening where you did not know what was going to happen next; that was what was good about it" (101).

Mailer extends his diatribe against drugs and his celebration of the glories of existential revolt to his discussion of the New Left, which "began with the notion that the authority could not comprehend not contain not finally manage to control any political action whose end was unknown." (102). But if the original idea of the New Left had its origins in the crude political aesthetic of the Cuban Revolution in which "you created the revolution first and learned from it" (102), by the time of the Pentagon march it was clear that accommodationism and coordinated planning were no longer being ignored. While in book 1 Mailer documents the rallies, the participants, his own clowning, and finally his celebrity arrest, in book 2 he shows the strategies of the protest movement, the logistics of the demonstration, and the drama of the confrontation itself. In fact, Mailer is suspicious of the New Left's willingness to compromise with moderate segments of the antiwar movement to avoid rupturing what was to say the least a fragile unity among a culturally and politically diverse coalition. Thus, conflicts between ultraradical leaders like Jerry Rubin and pacifist leaders like David Dellinger were, to Mailer's dismay, generally resolved in favor of the moderates.

Mailer's book is predominantly a meditation on the shortcomings of the New Left. The organizational character of the New Left causes Mailer to have doubts about its potential as a true revolutionary force; his solution is to exorcise all middle-class elements from the movement that make it weak, including destroying affiliations with liberal reformers, ethnic groups, and moderate women's and religious groups:

Left to him, he would have cut out all middle class protest movements like SANE and Women Strike for Peace because they derived, not genealogically he was certain, but spiritually, from the worst aspects of the American Communist Party, that dull old calculation that the apathetic middle class of America could be reached by middle class political organizations with middle class leaders and abstract Every man names like Women, Students, Artists, Professionals, Mothers, Veterans, Grand-mothers, yea why not Babes? [110].

Mailer thus perceives the dangers that coalitions with liberals may exert on the style and identity of the New Left. Better that "the new parties of the Left ... have names like motorcycle gangs and block athletic clubs had on their jackets: George Street Jumpers, and Green Dolphins, Orange Spar-rows, Gasoline Ghosts, Paragon A.C., Purple Raiders, Silver Dragons, Bug-house Beasts" (110), quips Mailer, though in his ironic analogy he overestimates the mob potential of street and motorcycle gangs, which, as has been seen, did not actually divest themselves of the codes and man-ners of the society they despised.

But while Mailer's charge that mediocre elements espousing civilized values cripple the primitive and thus explosive potential of countercul-tural protest is a compelling observation, it does little to undermine the drama of the march itself. Despite its overtones of rationalism, thousands were marching on the locus of totalitarianism. Terror infused both the demonstrators and the soldiers who surrounded the Pentagon, and the piquancy of the event had everything to do with the uncertainty of its out-come. It was unclear whether the Leftists were pivoted on the edge of dis-aster or were on the threshold of some marvelous new destiny. Indeed, Mailer's best writing in *The Armies of the Night* — those sections in which the special gifts of the novelist replace the documentary attributes of the historian — can be found in passages in which he observes the unexpected transformation of these weak, victimized children of the middle class into something resembling true warriors. As Jack Richardson has said, one of Mailer's great gifts has been to "turn often tedious and random happen-ings into interesting, cohesive speculation."[20] The Pentagon march was a primitive confrontation, the working-class soldier pitted against the mid-dle-class hippie, liberal, or politico from privilege: "In the midst of a tech-nological century, close to its apogee, a medieval, nay, a primitive mode of warfare was reinvigorated, and the nations of the world stood in grave observation."[21]

Ordinarily, for Mailer, it would be doubtful that these pampered dissidents from the middle class could transcend their fundamental mediocrity in the face of working-class ruthlessness as represented by the soldiers — the true primitives and underground heroes whom Mailer had often envied and celebrated in his writing. But this was a middle class inspired by a sense of being morally right, fiercely indignant in its belief that the Vietnam War was an atrocity. Moreover, it was a generation that had distinguished itself by its devotion to activism and whose central value was its zeal to confront power. "Standing against them, the demonstrators were not only sons of the middle class of course but sons who had departed the middle class, they were rebels and radicals and revolutionaries; yet they were unbloodied, they felt secretly weak, they did not know if they were the simple equal, man for man, of these soldiers" (285). The drama of the march, for Mailer, was precisely this clash of wills between the simple, lower-class soldier and his contemptuous opposite, the privileged but rebellious and personally alienated progeny of the middle class. These radicals were nothing less than a new social type, their energies galvanized by a radicalism that had entered the larger society. Would these angry rebels stand their ground, moral righteousness driving them to heights unexpected?

Many of Mailer's questions concerning the mettle of these unlikely combatants were answered when he wrote his sequel, *Miami and the Siege of Chicago* (1970). But the chaos that ensued in the confrontation between police and demonstrators at the Democratic Convention in Chicago might account, ironically, for the lesser impact of that book. The event was no less surrealistic than the Washington march had been, but its dramatic character was not so measurable or compelling because of the capacity of actual violence to overwhelm the novelist's instincts. The air of mysticism exuding from the Pentagon march, the unfolding of some new mass potential, the emergence of courage genuine enough to displace the lack of nerve that had characterized previous generations of the middle class, were all suddenly extinguished in the brutal police onslaught — an ugly and unfocused spectacle that distanced the observer and dissolved his keen sensitivity to nuance.

The spiritual and relatively benign elements of the Beat movement were absorbed by the countercultural movement of the 1960s, but as Mailer clearly documented, they took a back seat to egotism and aggressiveness when Beat impulses were politicized. "Once History inhabits a crazy house, egotism may be the last tool left to History," says Mailer (66). While other New Journalists backed off from the obvious implications, it was this primitive, confrontational aspect of the counterculture that intrigued Mailer, his own fascination with violence magnifying the meanings he attributed to its emergence. The march was of course only a prelude, a symbolic precursor to intensified upheavals and confrontations whose ego clashes would result in greater destruction, more brute force, and even death. But it was also a climax expressing the spirit of resistance whose rise had begun shortly after World War II to challenge the holy war being waged against political dissent by the most powerful men in America. It was the culmination of a profound, long-developing process of opposition as much as it was the outraged statement of a generation who opposed a war.

Most underground literature suffered from a variety of allegiances to a perceived audience in order to enhance its own interests or to protect itself from encroachment. Juvenile delinquent fiction had allegiances to a mainstream culture, but the Beat movement rapidly shifted the priorities of the popular novel to form an adversarial culture. The New Journalism signaled its allegiance to this new sensibility while at the same time it attacked elements that threatened it (Thompson and Sanders) or glorified that which enhanced it (Wolfe). In this complex period of history, the New Journalism was an honorable project, reflecting the adventurous spirit of the times, antagonistic to large forms of social control, and using new strategies to explain rapidly unfolding events. Yet it engendered its share of falsification due largely to the paradoxical relationship of its authors to an always shifting, often illusory and fragile political and cultural reality.

Ironically, the techniques of the New Journalism that intended to accommodate these shifts in the cultural climate, as often as not, worked against the genre. Personal testimony forced writers to be selective, if not in their modes of inquiry then at least in the presentation of their subjects. In this sense the New Journalism was as vulnerable as the old journalism, or any form of realistic writing for that matter, to sometimes preconceived, sometimes spontaneous attitudes anchored in more or less predictable political assumptions about the world, whether the politics be conservative (Wolfe), liberal-humanist (Sanders), or anarchist (Thompson).

Finally, perhaps the elusive nature of reality itself played a part in creating rational modes of subjectivity in the New Journalism. Mailer may be alluding to this when he confesses, "It may be obvious by now that a history of the march on the Pentagon which is not unfair will never be written any more than a history which could prove dependable in details" (289). Be that as it may, while at its worst the New Journalism was characterized by trendiness or by slick craftsmanship, at its best it was redeemed by the courage of its creators to adhere to radical action and personal involvement. It was the courage to seek out and to explore, and not its documentary accuracy, that ennobled and defined all underground writing from the beginning.

7

The Age of Monsters: Dominance and Submission in the Sixties

The undercurrent of violence existing in the various powerplays of the counterculture was clearly indicated in the best efforts of the New Journalists. Yet despite Tom Wolfe's assertion that only a literal report, and not fiction, could accurately reflect the bizarre events of the 1960s, the decade represented an absolute flourishing of the underground narrative — a sort of golden age for this fiction in the United States. It was in this period that Kesey's best work appeared, that Burroughs developed into a notable experimental novelist, and that *City of Night* and *Last Exit to Brooklyn* became best-sellers. Even Paul Bowles recaptured some of his old magic with his splendid 1968 potboiler *Up Above the World*.

And there was Grove Press. Burroughs's novels, as well as *City of Night* and *Last Exit to Brooklyn*, were published by Grove, a company that became synonymous with underground writing. Throughout the sixties, Grove and *The Evergreen Review*, its pioneering literary magazine, turned out the most dangerous work by the most provocative American and European writers of the past and present.[1]

Still, it is true that most underground fiction did avoid grappling with topical issues. Where was the novel of the Vietnam War? And what of the novel of campus revolt or of the Black Power movement? There were, of course, a few rare efforts to come to grips with these subjects. William Eastlake's *The Bamboo Bed* (1968) was one attempt to fictionalize the ill-fated U.S. involvement in Southeast Asia. Richard Farina's *Been Down So Long It Looks Like Up to Me* (1966), a minor underground classic about the stirrings of campus radicalism, presaged the public emergence of the New

Left, and Jeremy Larner's *Drive, He Said* (1970) was an interesting attempt to fictionalize campus revolt and misguided political idealism. Black writers came into their own in the 1960s, writing, as was characteristic of the time, autobiographical accounts of their harried lives in the ghetto and their struggle with racism. Eldridge Cleaver's *Soul on Ice* (1968) and *The Autobiography of Malcolm X* (1970) were notable products of the period.

But most underground fiction of the 1960s proved to be a refinement of the seminal visionary books of the 1950s, a further probing into areas of sexuality, psychic unraveling, and violence. The best of these fictions explored the dark, subversive world of life at the margins, as the best underground narratives always had, but the books suggested that the potential to transcend a corrupt society bent on oppression and control was becoming increasingly restricted. Many of these books remained underground in the truest sense, being appreciated by devoted cultists, and never reaching the mass popularity of fiction by writers who were embraced as heroes by the counterculture, writers such as Kurt Vonnegut and Thomas Pynchon. Perhaps it was the unprecedented nihilism of the books that kept them marginal. Dramas of interior chaos, their conflicts are often resolved by nihilistic withdrawal, madness, or sudden violence. And most important, they speak of the failure of countercultural energies at a moment when those who embraced the radical ethos sought to celebrate them.

Perhaps the most obscure of these underground writers was a man who, ironically, had played a significant role in authenticating underground fiction. Alexander Trocchi, a Scot from Glasgow, whom William Burroughs has called "a unique and pivotal figure in the literary world of the 1950s and 1960s,"[2] had established his credentials as a dedicated avant-gardist years before he produced any significant fiction. As a translator and editor at *Merlin*, a Paris-based literary quarterly, Trocchi published Samuel Beckett in English and later went to work for Maurice Girodias's Olympia Press. At Olympia, whose mission according to Girodias was to rebel "against ordinary logic, and ordinary good taste, and restraint and current morals,"[3] Trocchi translated Apollinaire, Georges Bataille, and the Marquis de Sade. It should be emphasized that the underground novel flourished at a time when the works of the Marquis de Sade could be found on drugstore book racks beside Von Krafft-Ebbing's *Psychopathia Sexualis*, Terry Southern's *Candy*, and Vladimir Nabokov's *Lolita*, the latter two having been first published by Olympia. Trocchi himself penned a series of pornographic novels for Olympia's Traveler's Companion series. His so-called Paris Novels, with titles like *Helen and Desire* and *White Thighs*, published under the pseudonym Frances Lengel, today read like mere paraodies of de Sade and Gide.

But even then Trocchi was much admired by those who knew him, generally perceived to be the most gifted writer of the Paris literary underground, and, according to Richard Seaver, the one "most likely to become our generation's Joyce or Hemingway or — more likely — Orwell."⁴ But Trocchi was also a man with a serious bent for self-destruction, having picked up a heroin habit, which significantly curtailed his literary production. He did, however, manage to create two masterpieces of underground fiction, *Young Adam* (1954) and *Cain's Book* (1961). Both novels reflect the vision of a nihilistic outsider who denies all transcendence to the individual and who seeks to explore a life of deliberate corruption. Trocchi's penchant for cultivating extreme attitudes can be summed up in a single statement typical of many he made during his lifetime: "I am outside your world and no longer governed by your laws."⁵

Young Adam, his first serious novel, was not published in the United States until 1960. Written in the early fifties, before Trocchi came to America —first to New York, then to Venice Beach, where he would become as legendary among members of the California wing of the Beat Generation as he was within the Paris literary underground — the book anticipated the passionate frankness that characterized his underground masterpiece *Cain's Book*. *Young Adam* was directly inspired by Camus's novel *The Fall*, with special leanings toward the kitchen-sink realism of the Angry Young Men, in the 1950s widely considered to be Britain's analogue to the Beat Generation. The novel is a curious hybrid — part pornography, part philosophical tract, and part social realism. The story involves the question of whether a young barge hand should reveal what he knows about an accidental drowning to clear a man who is falsely accused of murder, hesitating out of fear that he may himself be legally implicated in the woman's death. Kathie, the victim, in reality the narrator's mistress, a fact not known to the reader until half way through the book, becomes a real presence in the action, both as subject of debate on matters of life and death among the characters and as a source of reminiscence to the narrator. The narrator frequently replays incidents of sexual bravado, cruelty, and indifference concerning his dead mistress as he becomes more intimate with the barge captain's wife with whom he eventually has an affair. Like Camus's narrator in *The Fall*, he is uncertain about his responsibility for

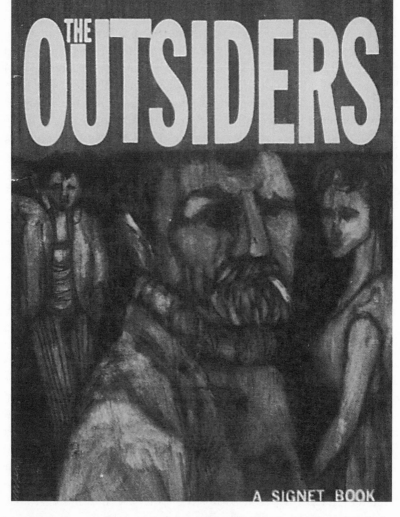

In an extraordinary new novel and four short stories, ALEXANDER TROCCHI, one of today's bold new writers, explores the tangled lives of men and women who live without roots or morals in a world where anything is acceptable. . . .

THE OUTSIDERS

D1905

A SIGNET BOOK

This 1961 Signet collection of Alexander Trocchi's work contained *Young Adam* as well as four short stories.

her death (he is not moved to rescue her when she topples into the river during a lover's quarrel but instead feels annoyance and "a kind of panic-tinged curiosity"). The narrator escapes into isolation and detachment: "It was pervaded with the unreality of fiction, dream. I would wake up soon. I had merely to walk away to free myself from an obsession."[6]

Nihilistic philosopher that he is, however, the narrator decides to let the innocent man go to the gallows, a move inspired as much by a hatred of the social system as by a bemused recognition of the absurdity of life. Irreverence, hatred of convention, and a cynical disdain for traditional values and morals were familiar traits in the work of the angry British writers like John Osborne, Stan Barstow, Kingsley Amis, and Alan Sillitoe. Confessing, the narrator says, "would have been, in an indirect but very fundamental way, to affirm the validity of the particular social structure I wished to deny."[7] The novel's atmosphere is redolent of most Angry Young Man novels, its details revealing the brooding, often stifling hardship of working-class existence and the search for joys, no matter how fleeting, to counter it: pubs at night, work on the barge by day, sexual encounters whenever possible — with Kathie, with Ella, and with Ella's stepsister, Gwendoline — form the stuff of the novel. None of these activities is fulfilling, but some ease the boredom.

Yet never is it suggested, as in many novels of the angry decade in Britain, that this character's rebellion can be, as Randall Stephenson has said of Angry Young Man literature, "quickly annulled by the acquisition of a job and a place in the world."[8] Trocchi's narrator in *Young Adam* is especially rootless, expressive of alienation and wanderlust that is in the end grounded in matters more metaphysical than social and that could only be found in the most pessimistic underground narratives. Trocchi seems to have taken special pleasure in depicting a disillusionment whose existence demands to be revealed. His isolation compels contemplation of dread and evil and a self-absorption that can find no relief in the ordinary things people do. Despite dwelling on his options as he follows the development of the innocent man's trial, Trocchi's narrator is bent on seeking relief in acts of deliberate corruption.

Existential violence of a different sort drives the stories of Michael Rumaker, who learned his craft under the tutelage of Charles Olson and Robert Creeley as a student at Black Mountain College in the early 1950s. His best stories, some written as early as 1954 for Olson's creative writing class, and most published as early as 1955 but not collected until Grove

Press's *Gringos and Other Stories* appeared in 1968, prophesy the public emergence of the Beats. Moreover, Rumaker's early fiction anticipated the currents of explosive violence that became characteristic not only of most underground writing in the 1960s but of many of the major public events that took place during the decade.

Rumaker examines collective violence and the special reality of society's dropouts. His stories form a virtual inventory of characterizations and themes that became the substance of the underground narrative. The subculture of juvenile delinquents in a fatalistic encounter with the police is dramatized in "The Truck," thieves and transvestites provide the theatrics in "The Bar," and footloose bums are the centerpiece of a meandering tale called "The Desert."

Two of Rumaker's most impressive stories, "Gringos" and "Exit 3," are road stories. "Gringos" features two drifters who spend a day in a Mexican bordertown drinking and whoring and finally brawling with Mexican bandits before venturing forth to destinations unknown. Rumaker reduces his characters to their essentials, blending them with their primitive environment, where instinct and reflex co-opt rational movement and purposeful action. "I ain't no gangster or nothing," says one character, Jim, "I'm walking away from trouble — at home — I always wanted to walk and see things — that's all."[9]

Even less pragmatic is the drunken marine in Rumaker's "Exit 3," a hitchhiker who needs to be restrained from persistent acts of senseless violence and self-destruction by a charitable sailor who ultimately fails to prevent the inevitable. In these stories the forces of resistance easily paralyze gestures of compassion and co-opt the standard of cooperation and community that characterized the spirit of the New Consciousness, from Black Mountain to Woodstock. And far from representing the road as a source of ecstasy and liberation, both of these stories attest to the chaos and social breakdown of the times, depicting the road as an unexamined wilderness of despair.

Certainly the story that most effectively captures the theme of violence as an expression of unfocused, inarticulate rage — violence as a reflex, an impulse almost as natural as breathing — is "The Pipe." It is in this story that Rumaker's wasteland setting of the mudflats along a river, over which extends a corrugated pipe periodically emitting dredge from the river's bottom, provides the closest connection between the desperation of the dispossessed and a compulsion to senseless violence. Six men hover over

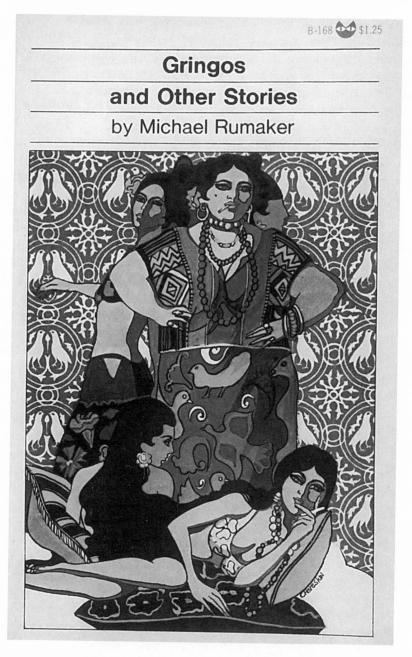

Gringos and Other Stories, Grove edition, 1968.

the rusted metal aperture to collect whatever detritus spews from the pipe that can be sold for scrap. As they wait for the periodic blast of filthy water to reveal what can be recovered, the men tell stories. One man, Billy, tells of a one-legged baby once having been found among the garbage washed out of the pipe. Despite the odd camaraderie that the men share, violence erupts from a senseless argument when Alex kills Sam by striking him with a metal flange. In the aftermath of violence, Alex accepts responsibility, and there is an atmosphere of compassion for the murdered man. But, as Rumaker made plain in "Gringos," the bottom dogs of society have cast their lot with their counterparts, other beasts animating the landscape, such as the wild dogs in the desert and, in this story, the hawks above, who circle the mayhem below. The shocking yet not wholly unexpected denouement of this story is perhaps the best illustration of Rumaker's theory that the writer must tap the unconscious when he writes. "The writer," Rumaker says, "must act upon the object in such a way that it gets said," and "the object must remain in its own context, as you, the writer, must also."[10] Perhaps this theory of his literary methods, containing elements of Charles Olson's celebration of an active process, is simply another way of regarding violence in America as a fact. Rumaker's stories present human aggression without resorting to easy explanations that might account for the origins of violence in human affairs.

If violence was indeed the final expression of hopeless men in an absurd universe, other notable underground fiction of the 1960s revealed the attempt by some to resist agents of control to avoid being consumed by the all-powerful system and to establish some advantage over others less adept at survival. Robert Stone's first novel, *A Hall of Mirrors* (1967), the decade's masterpiece of underground writing, is a powerful depiction of all that the oppositional milieu found wrong with America. Consistent with most underground narratives, the novel focuses on the lower-depth activities of the rootless who are unable to adjust to the demands of the powerful system. If other oppositional novels projected an intriguing but ideologically imprecise vision of society, Stone's book, like Ken Kesey's *One Flew Over the Cuckoo's Nest*, presents the terms of the conflict with a central horrific metaphor. Stone's setting of New Orleans functions, like Kesey's mental institution, as the locus of all the sickness of America. All those who stumble into its constricted atmosphere become enslaved by its machinations or fall victim to the corrupt power elite.

And the connection with Kesey is not a superfluous one. Stone moved to San Francisco in 1962 after being accepted into Stanford University's prestigious creative writing program. There, in Perry Lane, Stanford's bohemian quarter where Kesey himself had lived several years before, Stone began experimenting with psychedelic drugs. Stone was also a frequent visitor at close-by La Honda, often attending parties where Kesey, by then a successful novelist, conducted his LSD experiments. The drug experience undoubtedly left its mark on the brilliant, often surrealistic prose style of Stone's novel, which possessed a visionary quality it shared with Kesey's first book.

But unlike *One Flew Over the Cuckoo's Nest*, *A Hall of Mirrors* refuses to offer an escape from oppression in terms of freedom and the strength to oppose. The three central characters, each of whom has inclinations to break from the unfeeling system — Rheinhardt through his musical talent, Geraldine through her kindness and ability to love, and Rainey through his intense altruism — all fail to transcend the ruthlessness and mayhem of American life. Only Rheinhardt survives because he channels his failure into a nihilistic code that protects and removes him from control.

As the novel opens, Rheinhardt, the hero, has undergone a transformation from gifted Julliard music student to alcoholic social dropout. Having rejected family and a professional career, he has embarked on a life of wandering in which "the best times were the times wrapped in the haze of motion, of fields and mountains and sweeping towns, blackness and neon passing dreamlike over the droning of the motor."[11] He drifts into the city of New Orleans the day after Mardi Gras, possessing only sixty-five dollars, a gold watch, and a wedding ring. Stepping off the bus, he is questioned by a border patrol agent who mistakes Rheinhardt for a German immigrant, an unfavorable omen that anticipates the intimidating and oppressive circumstances to come.

Rheinhardt's down-and-out condition, which strips him of even the slightest hint of moral courage, compels him to grasp at any available opportunity. He soon gets a low-paying job at J. T. Bingamon's soap factory and then a well-paying one as an announcer on Bingamon's racist radio station, WUSA. Rheinhardt's advancement from alcoholic drifter to collaborator with racists is thus predominantly motivated by desperation — "I went in there a son of a bitch and I came out the same way except now I have some money and I'm eating shrimp" (119), he says after winning the job.

But, like Burroughs's characters, who attempt to remove themselves from either/or possibilities, Rheinhardt, cynical yet powerless to battle the system, needs to destroy the best that is in himself in order to remain aloof from the oppressors who reign triumphant over those who do not conform. Rheinhardt squelches his sensitivity and sense of social justice through indulgence in alcohol and marijuana but predominantly through a soulless and faceless bonding with the enemy. In this latter reincarnation he functions as a mere image, a reflection of the powerful destructive ideology he wants to escape. Insincere in his allegiance to powerful right-wing forces whose dangerous rhetoric he nonetheless espouses, Rheinhardt preserves his ability to transgress the transgressor: "Me, I'm a master of escape and I'm a master of disguise. When they force me to the water I'll devolve, man, I'll unevolutionize. I'll turn back into an amphibian" (147), he tells Geraldine, his lover, for whom he not surprisingly remains a mystery. Reducing all human activity to the level of a confidence game, Rheinhardt justifies his dubious actions with a bitter formula: "Unusual times demand unusual hustles" (147).

Not to invest one's energies in the monstrous system spells doom for the characters who hope to retain their humanity. Geraldine, the victim of abusive men, seeks salvation in love and companionship with Rheinhardt, with whom she is happy for a time. Meeting at the soap factory, Geraldine and Rheinhardt become lovers and settle in an apartment in the French Quarter, but eventually the relationship falls apart. Rheinhardt is too cynical to accept Geraldine's love and is moving in different directions; as he achieves status as media spokesmen for the right, Geraldine continues her downward spiral. The ultimate victim, once estranged from Rheinhardt she commits suicide in jail, having finally fallen into the clutches of the local police, who had already marked her as an undesirable as she entered the city at the outset of the narrative.

But salvation in love is not the only illusion dispelled in the novel. Morgan Rainey, welfare investigator, falls victim to his desperate desire to ease the suffering of humanity as he unwittingly becomes an instrument in a scheme by a corrupt politician named Minnow to get blacks thrown off of public relief. Rainey, whose charity and goodwill are matched only by Geraldine's, tries to strike up a relationship with her, but he is too much the vulnerable dreamer to succeed. Rainey's idealism is extreme and ultimately perceived by Geraldine as weakness, for he believes himself to be an extension of those with whom he sympathizes: "When they crush lives, they crush me. Their bombs destroy me. When men hang, I hang. When they flog women, they flog me" (274). Geraldine is too far gone to seek solace in one who identifies so intimately with other victims, and she reaffirms her devotion to Rheinhardt, the terrifyingly cool manipulator whose detachment allows him to rise above the corruption. Rainey dies in the end, being blown up in a truck filled with dynamite alongside S. B. Prothwaite, a terrorist who seeks to avenge himself on the menacing military and religious forces of the right at the pro-American rally that forms the climax of the novel.

It is in this section of the novel that Stone introduces a myriad of minor eccentric characters, all of whom bring the ideological conflicts to a boil. Though Stone's treatment is satirical, the characters reflect a sharp deepening of the moral chaos of the 1960s and portend a triumph for the right: the Reverend Orion Bunn of the Four Square Trinity church, "has amassed 24,000 signatures toward an initiative banning the teaching of the theories of Evolution" (287); Congressman Roscoe Chaplin's goal is nationwide censorship of "any book containing obscene words or plot as any situation of an adulterous or immoral character" (250); and Aldous Mars, a mysterious ex–CIA man, retains connections with secret sources of military intelligence.

It is also at the rally that the slippery, duplicitous Lester Clotho and Farley the Sailor reappear. Clotho, an apparently black entrepreneur who had been assigned to mislead Rainey in the welfare assault, reveals himself before Rainey to be white. Nor does he persist in masking his sinister self. The revelation engenders in Rainey a penetratingly clear vision of American deception: "Condolences, promises, guarded ridicule, seductions, false laughter — hysteria barely suppressed, panting violence, endearment, fear, unexpected passion, humiliation, polite cruelty, police deception — lies believed and lies unbelieved rose to his ears and died away" (319). Farley, another con man and traveler of the night who is always one step ahead of Rheinhardt, functions as Rheinhardt's alter ego. He is a cynical survivor with a track record of violence and madness behind him. As Brother Jensen of the Living Grace Mission, Farley is the catalyst for Rheinhardt's development as a demented radio evangelist.

Though the revival escalates into the violent riot anticipated by the Right shortly after Rheinhardt's address to the crowd at the stadium thronged by thousands, it falls short of the Armageddon hoped for by Prothwaite. Both Farley and Rheinhardt abruptly sever their alliance with the Right by beating up Bingamon, stealing his money, and making a hasty retreat. But Rheinhardt's victory over small-mindedness and bigotry turns out to be a hollow triumph. After learning of Geraldine's death, Rheinhardt seeks emotional refuge by intimidating the patrons of a bar. Attempting to assuage his grief in a half-serious Burroughs-like routine replete with accusations and suggestions of guilt, he resolves his conflicts by once again asserting his ruthless self: "'I'm a survivor,' Rheinhardt said, 'I'm full of self-confidence and I'm leaving the flats for Denver, the Mile High City'" (406).

Robert Solotaroff, a generally favorable critic of Stone's novel, tempers his praise with the suggestion that the relentless pessimism of the book is somewhat incompatible with the utopian spirit of the late sixties. "The novel's depiction of the violence, the social injustice, and the often sick sexuality of American life is not all that unfair to mid-1960s America, but the hopelessness, the apparent absence of experiential alternatives is."[12] Stone, however, has stated that he "was looking for a vision of America, for a statement about the American condition.... I wanted to be an American Gogol if I could, I wanted to write *Dead Souls*."[13] Moreover, as this study has shown, underground narratives, of which Stone's is among the finest, reveal a disturbing vision of moral and emotional chaos, seldom privileging the utopian ethos of the counterculture as it was projected by the media in the movement's mass-culture phase. Indeed, the title of Stone's novel captures the essence of the underground narrative as it was widely practiced, driving home its most consistent theme — that oppositional and subversive activities in the alternative milieu commonly reflect the ugliness of the system that is despised.

Simplistic notions of counterculture idealism and Beat joyousness had already been dashed in Jack Kerouac's *Big Sur* (1962) years before oppositional energies were harnessed into a mass youth movement. The breakdown of community and withdrawal into self were given full expression in one of Kerouac's most powerful novels, ostensibly depicting his three-week descent into despair, alcoholism, and madness while trying to recover his spiritual and mental well-being during an isolated retreat at Lawrence Ferlinghetti's cabin in Northern California. As John Tytell has written, "The book furthers the confessional mode of *The Subterraneans* and it correctly predicted the sorrow of his later years."[14] Indeed, the book is the most poignant example of Kerouac's breakdown, though others would follow. At the time of its publication, critics frequently compared the novel to F. Scott Fitzgerald's famous essay, "The Crack-Up," another autobiographical account of past failures and emotional instability that seemed to speak

Big Sur, Bantam edition, 1963.

with equal authority to the collapse of the romantic ethic for an earlier generation of lost bohemians. Yet Kerouac's book is not only a bitter meditation on the struggles of his professional life like Fitzgerald's; it is also a dark journey into the recesses of the self, consistent with such tragic and shattering chronicles of madness as August Strindberg's *The Inferno* and Sylvia Plath's *The Bell Jar*.

Despair, always present in Kerouac's vision but kept at bay through bouts of wild ecstasy as told in the great books of the 1950s, takes over here. Kerouac is revealed as a sadly disturbed personality, a greatly changed man from the one who labored fiercely over unpublished novels for years without recognition or reward. With the publication of *On the Road* and the hoopla that followed, fame had come fast, but Kerouac was not comfortable with his role either as a public figure or as a generational guru. His desire to escape from the limelight inspired reclusiveness and bouts of heavy drinking that affected his mood and his ability to write. Though *Big Sur* contains many of the emotional peaks and valleys that characterized his earlier books, a new tone of hostility and edgy bitterness dominates the narrative. And if the values that Kerouac once embraced in his classic books are present, they seem to exist primarily for the narrator to weakly reaffirm in a futile effort to stabilize his growing sense of unreality or to reject outright as ways of life that may no longer sustain him. It is as if Kerouac's purpose was to turn the world of *On the Road* upside down. Here, energy drifts into stasis, identification with the other turns into alienation, and companionship and opportunities for spiritual renewal become desperate bids to stave off madness.

Kerouac's narrator, Jack Duluoz, disillusioned "King of the Beatniks," is exhausted and unable to carry on with the things he once celebrated in his youth and his writing. Hitchhiking, for example, proves to be impossible. Making a trek to San Francisco after several weeks of painful isolation at Raton Canyon, Duluoz is passed on the road by numerous automobiles, most of which contain "the husband ... in the driver's seat with a long ridiculous vacationist hat with a long baseball visor making him look witless and idiot ... wifey, the boss of America wearing dark glasses and sneering ... and in the two deep backseats are children, children, millions of children, all ages, they're fighting and screaming over ice cream."[15] One discerns in anti-middle-class diatribes like this a sense of frustration rather than saintly glory in intelligent opposition that might have characterized Kerouac in his halcyon days.

Ultimately, fatigue besets him, and he resigns to complete his San Francisco trip by bus. Arriving at his destination, he visits old friend Cody (Neal Cassady), who is himself somewhat sapped by the years. Working in a tire shop, Cody is talkative and charming but markedly more reserved than in the old days. Yet it is eventually seen that Cody retains some of the old magic — still driving with skill, entertaining mistresses, and even sharing his latest girlfriend Billie with Duluoz, ironically exacerbating Duluoz's unstable mental condition. Sex, once a source of genuine liberation, fails to deliver, even becoming one more symptom of the illness and self-hatred that tortures Duluoz. After one intense bout of lovemaking with Billie, Duluoz describes his orgasm as an "empty feeling far from being the usual relief is now as tho I've been robbed of my spinal power right down the middle on purpose by a great witching force" (157).

But if human intimacy seems to be an extension of the pangs and pressures of celebrity rather than deliverance from it, Duluoz remains hopeful that contact with nature can yet restore him to spiritual health. Unfortunately, throughout the novel he is unable to find solace or communion in the wilderness, being frightened and intimidated instead of nourished by the sea, the wind, and the cliffs at Big Sur. Duluoz is occasionally peaceful but only "when I completely forgot who I was where I was or the time a day" (157). As in Burroughs, when the self is no longer absorbed by the activity, the ego runs wild, and a misuse of freedom results. Here the sources that previously inspired peace or spiritual contentment now generate aggressiveness and terror: "A whole mess of little joys amazing me when I came back in the horror of later to see how they'd all become changed and sinister" (25).

But it is not enough to realize that obliteration of the ego is necessary for him to return to health. Duluoz must also reestablish his connection with the physical world that frightens him, to interfuse the self with the natural environment around him. However, he remains distressingly aloof. The forest has "been there a million years and it doesn't want me clashing darkness with it." And the sea "didn't want me there, that I was a fool to sit there in the first place, the sea has its waves, the man has his fireside, period" (33). More frightening is his inability to confront the void and take any comfort in the reality of infinity, as any good Buddhist would. Kerouac had by this time, however, lost much of his interest in Buddhism[16]; thus, an atmosphere of impending death pervades the entire novel, and Duluoz recoils in horror at its inevitability.

Tormented by evil specters and the overwhelming indifference of nature, Duluoz desperately seeks consolation in the company of friends in San Francisco. Unfortunately, camaraderie leads to a drunken debauch that results in further distrust and alienation. The reunion with Pat McLear (Michael McClure), Ben Fagin (Philip Whalen), Dave Wain (Lew Welch), and Romona Swartz (Lenore Kandel), all young San Francisco poets, quickly deteriorates into paranoid suspicion, with Duluoz wondering whether they are "all a bunch of witches out to make me go mad."[17]

Feelings of persecution accelerate when Duluoz invites Billie to a party at the cabin. He hears voices, fears that Dave Wain is poisoning him with a needle he uses to take amphetamines, and that Billie, with her hateful, too curious son, her strange friends back in San Francisco, and her intense determination to marry him, is part of the conspiracy.

Duluoz's psychic disintegration is of course exacerbated by his constant drinking, which has given *Big Sur* status as a classic novel of alcoholism. Acute in its insight into its protagonist's harrowing struggle with the bottle, the book may be linked to such powerful drunk narratives as Jack London's *John Barleycorn* (1913), Charles Jackson's *The Lost Weekend* (1944), Malcolm Lowry's *Under the Volcano* (1947), Hans Fallada's *The Drinker* (1952), and Frederick Exley's *A Fan's Notes* (1968). Duluoz describes the delirium tremens as

> the feeling of standing ankledeep in hot boiled pork blood, ugh, of being up to your waist in a giant pan of greasy brown dishwater not a trace of suds left in it — the face of yourself you see in the mirror with its expression of unbearable anguish so hagged and awful with sorrow you cant even cry for a thing so ugly, so lost, no connection, whatever with early perfection and therefore nothing to connect with fears or anything. (4)

Though Kerouac's letters show that he had read and admired Lowry's *Under the Volcano* in 1951, a darkly revealing passage like the one above would seem to suggest that Kerouac had renounced the magic of white logic often attributed to the creative writer's need for alcohol. Kerouac, unlike most writers with alcohol problems, did not generally use alcohol as a source of inspiration for his writing — as a possible life-renewing agent. For his marathon writing sessions, he most frequently used Benzedrine to keep him going and occasionally marijuana as a stimulant, usually avoiding alcohol, a substance that could be antagonistic to the memory, which Kerouac relied heavily on to form the stuff of his literature. Alcohol, for Kerouac, functioned as a source to obliterate the world rather than to get in closer contact with it—an escape from despair, public pressure, and personal inadequacy. Following the media blitz that greeted the publication of *On the Road* and Kerouac's subsequent five-week binge that numbed him to the glare of publicity, Kerouac told John Clellon Holmes that alcohol was "my liquid suit of armor, my shield which not even Flash Gordon's super ray gun could penetrate."[18] Indeed, Kerouac's book is more consistent with a realistic novel such as *The Lost Weekend* than it is with a deeply symbolic and experimental one like Lowry's. As John W. Crowley has said of Jackson's novel,

> It is Jackson's refusal to amplify his material—to extrapolate from one drunkard's downfall to a symbolic utterance about the Tragedy of Life or the Decline of the West—that distinguishes *The Lost Weekend* from such grandiose modernist masterpieces as *Under the Volcano*. The force of Lowry's novel is centrifugal; it spins outward from its center (the Consul), traversing the cosmos as it accumulates layer upon layer of Higher Meaning. The force of *The Lost Weekend*, on the contrary, is centripetal; it turns in on itself toward a purposefully reductive focus on drinking, unadorned by any larger significance.[19]

Kerouac's offbeat impressionism stylistically distances him from Jackson's tough realism, but he is consistent with Jackson and other postwar writers in seeing alcoholism as an illness—in this case as a symptom, if not the actual cause, of the sickness that occupies him throughout the novel. Moreover, in a book that attempts to deglamorize, even destroy, the myths that had given Kerouac status as a writer for a new generation, it is not surprising to find that his need to derange the senses with excursions into drugs and alcohol has become a tragic personal burden rather than a vehicle to spiritual and artistic liberation.

The last thirty pages chronicle the depths of Duluoz's alcoholic misery in great detail. The writing ranges from additional horrific descriptions of delirium tremens—"your tongue is white and disgusting, your teeth are stained, your hair seems to have dried out"—to profoundly emotional ones—" you feel a guilt so deep you identify yourself with the devil"[20]—to a virtually clinical casebook rundown on binge phases, a day-by-day breakdown of steady drinking and developing horrors that culminate in a nightmare of sweating, physical pain, and hallucination.

Ironically, though Kerouac's talent was being extinguished in a sea of alcohol, most critics attribute the success of this book to its unity of purpose. Ann Charters has written, "In *Big Sur* he built his impressions of his experience into a coherently moving whole of richly visualized details all centering in his response to Bixby Canyon."[21] Indeed, Kerouac exerted a control over this novel that he sometimes abdicated when he seemed to merely report the experience rather than get to its psychological or mystical essence. Though Duluoz says at the conclusion, "I don't understand what happened at Big Sur even now,"[22] the book is extraordinarily adept at revealing the sources of the narrator's fear. The key to Kerouac's art had always been his extraordinary ability to empathize with his subjects, but to accomplish this he needed to limit his own involvement in the action. Here, however, he was himself the subject — center stage in a drama of uncertain and shifting identity. *Big Sur* is Kerouac's very own *Notes from Underground* but with saintly and vulnerable Prince Myshkin rather than the spiteful, unpredictable underground man as its protagonist.

His insecurity is often revealed when he retreats from the others to establish closeness with Cody's wife, Evelyn (Carolyn Cassady), the only person in the novel whom he seems to trust. Nor is Duluoz able to get much satisfaction from his achievement as a writer. He is impatient with the new generation, which idolizes him, and he has come to Big Sur to escape "the endless enthusiasms of new young kids trying to know me and pour out all their lives into me" (88). Yet there are several incidents in the narrative where he encounters young converts. On one hand Duluoz wants to reveal all of his shortcomings to them as if to preserve his actual identity, yet at the same time he is somehow afraid of disappointing his devotees by being an inadequate "King of the Beatniks." He usually opts to accommodate the legend. As a young teenager strums his guitar and sings his songs to Duluoz, the older man concedes, "I've got to make the best of it and not disappoint his believing heart" (88).

Other conflicts are more complex and painful. Duluoz is sensitive to the fallout with Cody, who has resented Duluoz's success with the novel that was based on him, and their friendship never regains its old firmness. *Big Sur* frequently tells of their mutual coldness, recalled in scenes in which neither has much to say to the other, such as the one in which the two share a joint and an uncomfortable silence ensues. And Duluoz's Catholicism is a curious foil to the hedonism with which he surrounds himself. "Satan is the cause of your alcoholism, Satan is the cause of your immorality, Satan is everywhere working to destroy you unless you repent now" (4), rants Duluoz, whose efforts to reform last no longer than the incantation itself and who fights his demons with his hypersensitive ego rather than yielding the riddles of his existence to God.

Though much of *Big Sur* reveals Duluoz's desperate attempt to connect with a reality outside the self, the book chronicles a painful alienation and portends his dispiriting rupture with a community that previously shared his own values and potential. The novel is a tragic document of a single man's mental collapse, but it presaged the terms for dissolution of an entire cultural movement years before either its utopian idealism or its ultimate fall would gain public attention. With the exception of *Desolation Angels* (1965), Kerouac would not write so well again. His last books continued the story of his personal decline but with a self-deprecating resignation that made them seem trivial. Yet his attack on the counterculture he had spawned grew ever more venomous, with public denouncements made during an embarrassing drunken appearance on William Buckley's television show, *Firing Line*, in 1968 and in a syndicated article attacking hippies and the antiwar movement called "I'm the Bippie in the Middle." His only visit to La Honda, at Cassady's invitation, was enough to make his fracture with the counterculture complete. Drunk and paranoid, Kerouac disapproved of the acid revelers, reproaching them for using an American flag to cover a sofa. LSD and the New Left were additional antagonisms to his increasing paranoia and conservative political outlook. But in retrospect it seems that Kerouac had the distinction of not only being the first to predict in direct terms the horrors to come, but with his early death in 1969 he was the first public figure to fall victim to its tragic contradictions.

More traditional novelists than those who perfected the underground narrative might have attempted to resolve the tensions between the individual and the other, as well as to reaffirm a social consciousness that could accommodate the jagged hedonism that Beat writers hoped would pump new vitality into American life. But because the entire Beat project was posited on its authors' establishing an authentic consciousness patterned on their actual lives, the work was faithful to perceived experience only, come what may. The vagaries and dilemmas of the self and the chaos that proceeded from it thus became emblems of the failure of this fellowship of resistance to achieve solidarity.

Still, the underground narrative maintained the integrity of a deeply subversive artistic activity. For Kerouac and for those writers whom he influenced and who would bring the underground narrative to a new level of brilliance in the 1960s, such honesty that was derived from the world they knew formed the basis of a significant oppositional literary art. And what the underground narrative lacked in terms of a consistent world-view, it made up for in its ability to capture the shifting character of the American mind during a time of great crisis. Remarkably, its most distinguished practitioners accomplished this task by using their own distraught consciousness as a primary source.

Conclusion

The powerlessness of the individual lost in a vast, complex, corporate society is a major theme in postwar American fiction. As the fates of many antihero protagonists of these fictions reveal, the seeking of new areas of energy to generate individuality and a sustaining value system is often a desperate and self-defeating search.

The underground narrative tested society's powerful challenge to the individual by celebrating not only new sources of energy but also new sources of power. Underground fiction constituted resistance to the technological, military, industrial, and political forces at large by asserting adversarial values and by exploring human potential in desperate acts of freedom. Flouting social and sexual mores was one strategy, but the larger purpose was to advance the notion that defiance of society might best be accomplished by creating a new lifestyle that others could share. Eventually, as the counterculture and the New Left surfaced, visibility in numbers promised to be a solution — but to go on the offensive was only possible if a revolution of consciousness occurred.

This utopian desire for gemeinschaft in the midst of mass society — an alternative to it — most specifically constituted a program to recover the lost self that many writers believed society had been long in the process of wearing away. Acknowledging powerlessness and discovering a way of transcending it presented a problem for the underground writer, but hope for salvation was immensely complicated by the contradiction inherent in his solution. The writer who imagined liberation through membership in a community that vastly reduced the opportunities for expression of the individual self was faced with a problem arising from his becoming a selfless collaborator with others who presumably shared his values. The conflict between those enacting assertions of self, which required visible and dramatic risk beyond social controls, would be frequently repeated in subcultural rituals, often creating breakdown within the subculture itself.

The popular novel was ideally suited to capture themes related to institutional corruption, youthful aggression and conflict, as well as to express the kinds of controversial subject matters that preoccupied many writers during the period. Collective insurgency first came to be noticed in the juvenile delinquent potboilers of the late 1940s. But the cultural impact of ritualistic defiance hinted at in writers like Motley, Shulman, Ellison, etc. was deflated by the fatalism inherent in the root material. In naturalism, the primary inspiration for these works of heightened real-ism, the sense of doom and self-destruction overpowers any real threat to society. Of course the dismissal of juvenile delinquents as viable threats to society began in smugness but would be modified as the genre responded to a pervasive and visible youth culture. Thus the range of response by those who speculated on the gang phenomenon and its effects on cultural and social order fluctuated from farce to tragedy. Yet the tendency to see the will to challenge and to violate the laws of a civilized society as being limited in its impact was in fact the consistent and relatively prophetic view held by many authors in the genre responding to cultural insurrec-tion even as the underground became a perceptible and seemingly viable alternative.

The response to such rational fatalism was, however, provided by the Beats, who were open to the possibility of radical, unbridled self-devel-opment and who sought to capture it in a return to American idealism. Resisting naturalism because it led to victimization, they resorted to other no less literary sources, though they were less pragmatic and doom-filled ones than naturalism: specifically, to transcendentalism, particularly the openness to nature and to experience found in Emerson, Thoreau, and Whitman; to the visionary extravagance of William Blake; to the existen-tial tradition, which focused on developing the self outside of traditional standards set by society, religion, or law begun in Dostoyevsky and con-tinuing through Sartre and Camus; and to Surrealism, which challenged the primacy of logic to answer the difficult questions facing the self. Add to this a strong impulse to protest and activism, and Beat writing pre-sented a most unusual combination of the pastoral and the urban.

In its earliest stages the urban element was pervasive in Beat writing, and European models, particularly Dostoyevsky and Sartre, prevailed. Self-analysis and intense dramatizations of what Holmes called "extremes of conviction" were the stuff of Holmes's and Brossard's confessional narratives. Yet despite the concentration on self, there is at the same time in both *Go* and *Who Walk in Darkness* a retreat from the self, a willingness to embrace that which is outside of it. The rationalism of the narrators of both novels is challenged by impulses toward the irrational, the swing toward disorder inspired by the community of drifters with which they maintain peripheral interest. A sort of effacement of the old self results from a reluctant fascination with the other — the amoral other who harkens back to the American tradition found in the common, the rough, the extraordinary, or in this case, in the new, which reaffirms American faith in the possibility of renewal.

While Holmes and Brossard finally distanced themselves from the powerful outsider model, Jack Kerouac, who was more comfortable with hero worship and a muting of his own persona in his fiction, articulated the appeal of adhering to the way provided by the individual, who for Kerouac might spearhead the new cultural order. In Neal Cassady, a primitive from the lower classes, Kerouac found the archetype. Subsequently, Kerouac created in *On the Road* the apt vehicle to celebrate the liberating figure, his novel a paean to individualism, its narrator joyful in the rapt exuberance of his observations and uncritical of the hero's excesses. Kerouac revived the tradition of the sociopath as a major cultural type — revered for his pathological zeal to remain totally free.

Ken Kesey imitated and refined Kerouac's literary strategies by inventing a larger hero than Kerouac's Dean Moriarty in Randall Patrick McMurphy, who suggests powerful, rampant individualism not so much as a model to aspire to but as a figure of menace. McMurphy is no less than an agent of retribution on an increasingly bland and mechanical society — a force presumably capable of generating not just cultural but political revolution. As the counterculture formed and assimilated many of the ideals inherent in the books of Kerouac and Kesey, it was clear that what was literary, designed by intellectuals using very specific American archetypes and values to form its substance, had in fact become a path to a new way of living. Not surprisingly, Kesey, after writing his novel *Sometimes a Great Notion* (1964), abandoned literature in order to manifest and develop the cultural energies he had helped bring into being. Kesey, like Kerouac, was a self-creation, a powerful force in the counterculture who understood his ability to create myth and see it borne out in terms of celebrity. And it was indeed this celebrity created by exposure to the media that had always sustained the Beat movement. Even in the early stages of the movement the Beats were more than just writers; they were superb media manipulators who knew how to gain the attention of their audience and form the right allegiances and antagonisms. Public exposure allowed the Beats' message to transcend its actual value as literature, though in Kerouac, Burroughs, and a few others the achievement was indeed genuine, and to promote its most necessary virtues: spontaneity, truth, and renewed consciousness. Perhaps only its open-endedness, its function as a fugitive literature, and its inherent skepticism could allay the contradictions and tensions of a movement that cherished both the values of community and individuality at the same time. Yet, as community became synonymous with commercialism, Kerouac and Kesey retreated into isolation, both aware that the substance of their idealism had been usurped and diluted by the very forces that had assisted its rise.

But the contradiction between selflessness and extreme self-assertion was further exacerbated by the incompatibility of the root materials by which spiritual resolution was sought and the historical moment that made such a quest desirable. For Whitman spiritual development and technological advancement were inseparable elements in a program to achieve democratic unity. But in the postwar period these elements were antagonistic and generated alienation rather than solidarity. Moreover, for those like Kerouac and Kesey, who conceived escape in traditional terms by returning to nature and to the notion of Emersonian perfectibility, the burden on the self was enormous. Kerouac and Kesey's books suggest a defiance of limitation. The return to space and to nature is finally a failure, as in Kerouac, or an unconvincing dream, as in Kesey. Yet the quest for renewal is never forsaken, though new and more desperately inventive vehicles must be imagined as their protagonists continue to be at odds with society. Domination, aspirations to control, and violence are the usual stances; drugs, wild acts of liberation, and further withdrawal into aggressive but impersonal sex are the typical vehicles. Characters in their books, always on the edge, lose control because their activities, primarily adversarial and, at least in Kesey's case, confrontational, require compounded risk. Despite their inherent idealism, Kerouac and Kesey's visions were ultimately doom-filled because in conceiving their fictions as celebrations of a great lost freedom they signaled repeatedly the inevitable failure of the attempt to recover it — in self-destruction, physical and psychic exhaustion, confrontational carnage,[1] or in more subtle forms of disempowerment through cultural and commercial assimilation.

But the tradition of American individualism is nonetheless stubbornly persistent throughout the underground narrative. In no other genre is the inability of the American hero to be selfless at work more tragically than in the gay novel. The failure to abandon the ego and thereby to engage in meaningful self-discovery here dooms the possibility of transcendence through love or community. Because the gay underground picaro perceives his sexuality as an extreme act of freedom and seeks to enlarge the self, he must pay a terrible price. He loses connection to all that may sustain him in the world and instead becomes imprisoned in the self — fearful, angry, and isolated.[2]

Yet, as the drug novel has shown, alienation and personal development, though generating isolation from community, might at least be viable ways of rebelling against a totalitarian order by providing an alternative way of life in an enclosed world, the self inviolable in the face of oppression. Transcendence through drug stimulation had been endorsed by the Beats, who also practiced other means of turning inward to achieve self-knowledge, including Buddhism. But most fiction about drug addiction emphasizes its destructive side. In Algren's *The Man with the Golden Arm*, addiction becomes a metaphor for cultural disintegration, and the novel is perhaps the most elegiac of his works. Burroughs is less sentimental in his diagnosis of the drug subculture, but he too announces its extinction. In Burroughs all hopes of finding solace or expression in subcultural activities are annihilated. And while he rules out the option of escape through drugs or movement and signals the death of community, he leaves open the possibility of finding refuge in an egoless self or escape into image that reduces vulnerability and subsequently provides protection from the other.

Burroughs's fictions forecasted the death knell on countercultural potential and protest. But they also dramatized the nightmare that the idealisms and paradoxes of underground writing so convincingly foreshadowed, as ego and power, weapons employed to support the conflict, superseded all other values of subcultural idealism. New Journalism, a strategy focusing on underground activities, or to be more precise, that which was off-center in American life, sought to document what some journalists like Tom Wolfe believed fiction was no longer able to deal with. But the New Journalism, in its celebration of the here and now, sounded a cautionary note. Its major works took on as subject those aspects of American life that were unique but threatening, symptomatic of the erosion of sub-cultural energies and presumably the underground's newfound power.

The analysis was revealing: erosion through commercialism in Wolfe's *Electric Kool-aid Acid Test*; the presence of fascistic elements represented by the Hell's Angels, who used self-promotion to achieve recognition and countercultural sympathy in Thompson's *Hell's Angels*; protest through direct assault on the mainstream society in Ed Sanders's *The Family* by cult leader Charles Manson, the murderous messiah whose attack literalized and consequently magnified countercultural aggression, politically con-sistent with the spirit, though not the actual activities, that was central to subcultural defiance.

Such were the symptoms exposed by writers who were reluctantly charting the counterculture's demise. These books were hastily written, their authors not fully aware of the implications of their materials. Nonetheless, seen in retrospect, they are books that clearly document a threat to the continuation of the counterculture whose unique power had always been located in a precarious realm dividing ecstatic transcendence from self-indulgent disaster. A testament to its demise was provided, fittingly, by Hunter S. Thompson himself. The ideal of self-indulgence for purposes of transcendence was trashed in his *Fear and Loathing in Las Vegas* (1972), the story of Thompson and his attorney's journey in a rented car to Las Vegas to cover a motorcycle race for *Sports Illustrated*, the entire time spent in drug-induced psychosis. Originally appearing in *Rolling Stone Magazine* in two lengthy installments in the November 11 and 25, 1971 issues, the piece prompted editor Charles Perry to comment, "After reading it, nobody with a straight face could talk about psychedelics as being essentially a religious experience."[3]

It is a distinct lament that these books now seem to intone. Many underground writers were disenthralled, often recoiling at the tragic con-sequences of the revolt their idealism had inspired. With self-abandon-ment being central to the underground's appeal and practice, it can be said that the seeds of the underground's dissolution were contained within its program of liberation. It is this idea that is played out in the nihilistic mas-terpieces of the underground narrative in the 1960s.

Lacking a true communal ethic or theory, the counterculture foundered in the early seventies and reached virtual distinction by mid-decade. Stoddard Martin describes the fall from idealism:

> Post-war dreams of literary cenacles in London, New York, and
> San Francisco, with their neo-Surrealism, their New Romantic,
> New Apocalyptic, and "beat" labels, led to an interlude of civil-
> rights activism, pacifism disarmament crusades, hippyism, drug
> expansion, environmentalism, gay liberation, and a general
> rebellion against the coersions of institutional psychology. But
> that long summer afternoon of freedom came to its autumn in
> the mid 1970s, a "selfish" period in which the youth of the mid-
> dle classes turned towards the comforts of elitist privilege.
> America is where this turnabout happened most distinctly.[4]

Perhaps it is more accurate to see this "selfish period" not as contradiction, turnabout, or reversal — a reaction to failed '60s idealism — but
as a continuation of the individualism to its more natural ground. Indeed,
by the 1980s the novel of marginal excess was transformed into the novel
of privileged excess with Jay McInerney's *Bright Lights, Big City* (1984),
and especially Bret Easton Ellis's *American Psycho* (1991). The latter, reminiscent of Hubert Selby Jr.'s *The Demon* (1976), which also has as its protagonist a man who is materially successful yet compelled to commit
depraved acts and violent crime, is in many ways a fitting coda to the string
of underground narratives discussed in this book. If Selby's novel, its energies inspired by quintessential Beat imperatives, somewhat abstractly sat-
irizes the American dream and the inadequacy of material goods, domestic
bliss, and professional contentment to contain the evil in human nature,
Ellis's novel is intimately connected with '80s superficiality and materialism — a lament for a decadent youth culture gone to seed from overindul-
gence in sex, drugs, and money. In addition to detailing the obnoxious
social codes of his characters, Ellis heaps generous doses of obscenity and
violence onto his narrative, illustrating through his protagonist, Patrick
Bateman, the familiar dynamic of power that reflects the asociality and
individualistic aggressiveness of the bourgeois world he is attacking.
Whether dramatizing the difficulties encountered by those who choose an
adversarial code of ethics to separate themselves from the society they
abhor, or satirizing the superficiality of style and the emptiness of material success in yuppie journeys into terrifying freedom, the underground
narrative served as a harsh reality check.

Though one of the purposes of this study has been to show the impact
of the Beats on specific writers who followed them, it would be misleading to insist on the Beat movement's estrangement from general trends in
American fiction during the postwar period and beyond. Indeed, it can now

be seen that Beat literature reflected many of the concerns that affected all writers of the period, rejecting the faltering moral certainties of the forties that informed the social novel. Beat writers also shared most postwar writers' attempts, including black and Jewish writers, to transform fiction from prewar ambitions of politically engaging large social issues to a type of fiction concerned with a personal view of life, assigning authenticity to individual solutions to alienation. As I have shown, Beat writers shared the longing to return to human connection, paving the way for the new romanticism of the homoerotic tradition, whose most politically significant work was produced in the sixties. Yet in its intimations of nihilism, Beat writing informed many formal experiments characterizing postmodern writing in the seventies forecasted by Burroughs and, to some extent, by New Journalism.

Above all, Beat literature remains a fascinating literary phenomenon, the solitary aesthetic gesture during a repressive and anesthetized age to combat intolerance, naive pro-Americanism, and conservative politics. Though its emphasis on individualism inhibited its potential for effective social involvement, its anger and bitter revolt against narrow-minded bourgeois values and tepid liberalism made it an archetypical American oppositional literature. The underground narrative, despite its evangelical nature and emphasis on cultural obstinacy and politics grounded in lifestyle — its aversion to ideology and collective political forms of revolution — proved to be a parallel gesture of dissent, even, in its own way a successor to the radical tradition of dissent that has characterized so much American literature of this century. Moreover, it posed new challenges in the name of identity and community to a rigidly monolithic culture. Thus it was an essential precursor to multiculturalist postmodern trends because of its insistent focus on previously ignored subject matters and on communities existing outside the mainstream society. The underground preceded and anticipated much fiction today that concerns the lives of outsiders and their quest to achieve identity.

Though the mainstream press has insisted that we are currently in the midst of a Beat revival, interest in the central writers of the Beat Generation has in fact been abundant and consistent. Gregory Stephenson has attributed their continuing appeal to a "quality of authenticity. We respond to the truth of their writing because we feel that they were created out of real pain and hope, out of absolute personal necessity."[5] Indeed, in their zeal to tell the truth, even the most utopian underground writers deconstructed the process of celebration recounted throughout their narratives; idealization of the human spirit was checked by evidence of ugliness and dark aggression within the underground milieu itself. To its credit, the fiction of the underground rang with dark prophecy, fearless in its realism.

But if the Beats have achieved popular appeal, critical acceptance has come hard. Since the 1970s various studies and biographies of major Beat figures have been produced, though academic trends have generally proven hostile to underground writing. But structuralist and poststructuralist theories created out of purely literary considerations have not been suitable methods to evaluate such writing; cerebral academic disciplines are simply too narrow in their methodologies to provide insight into fiction that attempted to provide more than solitary aesthetic pleasure and whose very existence depends on the living presence of the author in every phase of the text. Only Burroughs, the great avatar of the postmodern, is valued because his often impenetrable fiction flashes with conscious awareness of language's traps and limitations. Ironically, Burroughs's self-consciousness was generated from deeply personal imperatives and not by any inclinations to theorize about the artistic object. Rather, as in the work of other underground writers, Burroughs's methods were employed in an effort to effect radical cultural change.

So it is perhaps the destiny of underground fiction to remain popular with the intelligent reader who connects with the work in the deepest, most personal ways and not with the professional critic who is most concerned with assessing it. As Seymour Krim says about the readership of one of the early influences on the underground, Thomas Wolfe,

> They did not, and apparently still do not, care that his books are not "well-made" or that the author under another name is the hero of each. What they do care urgently about is what these books make them feel; how the intensity of Wolfe's quest carries past the page into their own lives and stirs them as no other American novelist of the same period can do.[6]

Perhaps the most formidable legacy of underground writing is that in its attempt to equate art with life it helped to shatter the elitist, hierarchical basis of the old highbrow culture.

Despite the ongoing popularity of the fictions themselves, the seventies, the eighties, and the nineties may be characterized more by a spirit of caution than by unrestrained desire for liberation, and the no-holds-barred journey to self-discovery celebrated in so many postwar novels is undervalued, even distrusted in more recent fiction. Indeed, there seems little of cultural consequence in the senseless mayhem of gang warfare, and the specter of AIDS has done little to encourage full expression of one's unconscious through sexual promiscuity and drug abuse.

Our desire to find answers to the baffling questions of our time has finally made us less willing to embrace the paradoxes that accompany the excesses of underground narratives. And it should be emphasized that paradox is writ large in such fiction. Specifically, though members of the underground attempted to escape from the bourgeoisie, their celebration of alternative mythic possibilities eventually became fashionable enough to be practiced by even the most mundane elements of society for whom experimentation became little more than chic style. And as idealistic and hopeful as much underground writing was, it was ultimately apocalyptic in its implications; as much as it embraced the value of the individual, it recognized the folly of pursuing individualistic goals at the expense of abandoning community; as much as motion and community were cele-brated, stasis and loneliness were just as often invoked; and even though it placed importance on human identity, it eventually turned to role-play-ing as a form of protection.

Throughout this study I have often dealt harshly with such paradox, particularly when human or moral reference has been breached in the ser-vice of the antimonian principle. But perhaps in the end these paradoxes really need not be resolved, for the search for freedom must often engen-der paradox, its ends defined by the activity itself. As John Rechy has said, "The search is the end — not the answer — the riddle. The ultimate life-hunt, without object. Everything is found in nothing."[7] And, as existence has no parameters, the search for life-giving values engaged by literary artists will go on.

Yet, as I think this study has shown, what began as a literary move-ment with roots in native traditions ultimately transcended art to become a distinct social and cultural force — for the most part, a behavioral exper-iment rather than an aesthetic one. Indeed, there was a time during the sixties in the shift from a moralistic to a tolerant society when anything seemed possible. But if that time and that sentiment are remote now, part of a naive past, it should be remembered that the wish for renewal and fulfillment is not exclusively cultural or a uniquely American preoccupation but a universal human impulse; in the gulf between imagination and desire and they way things are, we are eternally driven to grope towards redemptive values. It was the hope of discovering such values and the longing to put them to use that fueled the ambitions of underground writers and ultimately accounted for the impact of their work.

The Underground
Narrative: A Chronology

Though it can be argued that the works of the decadents of the late nineteenth century — those by Baudelaire, Wilde, and Huysmans — and especially Dostoyevsky's *Notes from Underground* (in many ways the first modern underground novel) were important forerunners of the underground narrative, underground fiction was primarily a twentieth-century phenomenon and particularly American in its concerns with the self and with aggressive individuality. Still, I have included here a few continental works that were directly influential (or should have been had they been better known) on the underground writers after the war, most of which contain taboo or archetypal underground subject matter and/or an almost hysterical sense of personal alienation and hostility to bourgeois codes of conduct. This list contains only fiction and not the various nonfictional works that have been referred to throughout this book. However, an autobiographical and confessional bent — a sense of personal urgency — can be found in most works linked to the phenomenon.

1902	*The Immoralist*, Andre Gide
1903	*Tonio Kroger*, Thomas Mann
1905	*The Little Demon*, Fyodor Sologub
1906	*The Road*, Jack London
1907	*Sanine*, Mikhail Artsybashev
1910	*The Notebooks of Malte Laurids Brigge*, Rainer Maria Rilke
1914	*Lafcadio's Adventures*, Andre Gide
1915	*The Rainbow*, D. H. Lawrence
1918	*The Inferno*, Henri Barbusse
1919	*Demian*, Hermann Hesse
1922	*Diary of a Drug Fiend*, Aleister Crowley
	The Pit, Alexander Kuprin

1925	*The Trial*, Franz Kafka
1926	*Moravagine*, Blaise Cendrars
	The Sun Also Rises, Ernest Hemingway
	You Can't Win, Jack Black
	Jarnegan, Jim Tully
1927	*Steppenwolf*, Hermann Hesse
	My Life and Loves, Frank Harris
1928	*Nadja*, Andre Breton
	Perversity, Francis Carco
1929	*Look Homeward, Angel,* Thomas Wolfe
1930	*Bottom Dogs*, Edward Dahlberg
	Poor Fool, Erskine Caldwell
1932	*From Flushing to Calvary*, Edward Dahlberg
	Journey to the East, Hermann Hesse
	Journey to the End of the Night, Louis Ferdinand Celine
	Young Lonigan, James T. Farrell
1933	*The Young and the Evil*, Parker Tyler and Charles Henri Ford
1934	*Tropic of Cancer*, Henry Miller
	Finnley Wren, Phillip Wylie
1935	*Waiting for Nothing*, Tom Kromer
	Of Time and the River, Thomas Wolfe
1936	*Nausea*, Jean Paul Sartre
	Death on the Installment Plan, Louis Ferdinand Celine
1939	*Tropic of Capricorn*, Henry Miller
	Ask the Dust, John Fante
1941	*The Journal of Albion Moonlight*, Kenneth Patchen
	Reflections in a Golden Eye, Carson McCullers
1942	*The Stranger*, Albert Camus
1943	*Our Lady of the Flowers*, Jean Genet
1945	*Memoirs of a Shy Pornographer*, Kenneth Patchen
	The Air-Conditioned Nightmare, Henry Miller
1946	*The Neon Wilderness*, Nelson Algren
	Sleepers Awake, Kenneth Patchen
	The Fall of Valor, Charles Jackson
1947	*The Amboy Dukes*, Irving Shulman
	Knock on Any Door, Willard Motley
1948	*The City and the Pillar*, Gore Vidal
	The Future Mr. Dolan, Charles Gorham
	The Naked and the Dead, Norman Mailer
	Other Voices, Other Rooms, Truman Capote
1949	*Duke*, Hal Ellson
	The Man with the Golden Arm, Nelson Algren
	Quatrefoil, James Barr
	Sexus, Henry Miller
	The Sheltering Sky, Paul Bowles
	The Thief's Journal, Jean Genet
1950	*The Town and the City*, Jack Kerouac

1951	*Barbary Shore*, Norman Mailer
	The Catcher in the Rye, J.D. Salinger
	Finestere, Fritz Peters
	Parent's Day, Paul Goodman
	Cassidy's Girl, David Goodis
1952	*A Cry of Children*, John Horne Burns
	Flee the Angry Strangers, George Mandel
	Go, John Clellon Holmes
	Let It Come Down, Paul Bowles
	Who Walk in Darkness, Chandler Brossard
	The Corpus of Joe Bailey, Oakley Hall
1953	*The Bold Saboteurs*, Chandler Brossard
	Junky, William Burroughs
	The Outsider, Richard Wright
1954	*The Blackboard Jungle*, Evan Hunter
1955	*The Deer Park*, Norman Mailer
	Pickup, Charles Willeford
	White Thighs, Alexander Trocchi
	Lolita, Vladimir Nabokov
1956	*Giovanni's Room*, James Baldwin
	Rock, Hal Ellson
	A Walk on the Wild Side, Nelson Algren
	The Fall, Albert Camus
1957	*On the Road*, Jack Kerouac
	The Ginger Man, J. P. Donleavy
	The Temple of Gold, William Goldman
	Some Came Running, James Jones
1958	*The Deadly Streets* (stories), Harlan Ellison
	The Dharma Bums, Jack Kerouac
	The Horn, John Clellon Holmes
	Rumble (a.k.a. *Web of the City*), Harlan Ellison
	The Subterraneans, Jack Kerouac
	The Golden Spike, Hal Ellson
	Candy, Maxwell Kenton
	Doctor Sax, Jack Kerouac
1959	*Crazy October* (stories), James Leo Herlihy
	Naked Lunch, William Burroughs
1960	*The Black Book*, Lawrence Durrell
	The Breakwater, George Mandel
	Cain's Book, Alexander Trocchi
	The Scene, Clarence L. Cooper
	Shake Him Til He Rattles, Malcolm Braly
	Tristessa, Jack Kerouac
	All Fall Down, James Leo Herlihy
	Ritual in the Dark, Colin Wilson
1961	*The Outsiders* (stories, including the novel *Young Adam*), Alexander Trocchi

1961	*The Soft Machine*, William Burroughs
	Pinktoes, Chester Himes
	The American Express, Gregory Corso
	Stranger in a Strange Land, Robert Heinlein
1962	*Big Sur*, Jack Kerouac
	One Flew Over the Cuckoo's Nest, Ken Kesey
	The Butterfly, Michael Rumaker
	The Ticket That Exploded, William Burroughs
1963	*City of Night*, John Rechy
	V, Thomas Pynchon
1964	*A Hall of Mirrors*, Robert Stone
	Last Exit to Brooklyn, Hubert Selby Jr.
	Nova Express, William Burroughs
	Sometimes a Great Notion, Ken Kesey
	Get Home Free, John Clellon Holmes
	Summer in Sodom, Edwin Fey
1965	*An American Dream*, Norman Mailer
	Desolation Angels, Jack Kerouac
	The Warriors, Sol Yurick
1966	*Been Down So Long It Looks Like Up to Me*, Richard Farina
	It's Cold Out There, Malcolm Braly
1967	*You Didn't Even Try*, Philip Whalen
	Numbers, John Rechy
1968	*Gringos and Others Stories*, Michael Rumaker
	Red-Dirt Marijuana and Other Tastes, Terry Southern
	Up Above the World, Paul Bowles
	The Real Thing, William Carney
1969	*Notes of a Dirty Old Man*, Charles Bukowski
	Street of Stairs, Ronald Tavel
	Memoirs of a Beatnik, Diane DiPrima
	This Day's Death, John Rechy
1970	*Cruisin'*, Gerald Walker
	The Mad Cub, Michael McClure
1971	*The Adept*, Michael McClure
	Post Office, Charles Bukowski
	The Wild Boys, William Burroughs
	Wake Up. We're Almost There, Chandler Brossard
	The Room, Hubert Selby Jr.
1972	*Dog Soldiers*, Robert Stone
	The First Third, Neal Cassady
	Visions of Cody, Jack Kerouac
1973	*A Good Day to Die*, Jim Harrison
	Exterminator, William Burroughs
	The Fourth Angel, John Rechy
1975	*The Last Words of Dutch Schultz*, William Burroughs
1976	*The Demon*, Hubert Selby Jr.
1978	*Requiem for a Dream*, Hubert Selby Jr.

1978	*Ladies Man*, Richard Price
	Incandescence, Craig Nova
1979	*Rushes*, John Rechy
1981	*My First Satyrnalia*, Michael Rumaker
	Cities of the Red Night, William Burroughs
1983	*Bodies and Souls*, John Rechy
	Ham on Rye, Charles Bukowski
1984	*Bright Lights, Big City*, Jay McInerney
	The Place of Dead Roads, William Burroughs
1985	*Less Than Zero*, Brett Easton Ellis
	Queer, William Burroughs
	Waiting for the End of the World, Madison Smartt Bell
1986	*The Last Museum*, Brion Gysin
	Demon Box, Ken Kesey
	Song of the Silent Snow (stories), Hubert Selby Jr.
1987	*The Western Lands*, William Burroughs
1989	*Wild at Heart*, Barry Gifford
	Interzone, William Burroughs
1990	*Homeboy*, Seth Morgan
1991	*American Psycho*, Brett Easton Ellis
1992	*Moloch: or This Gentile World*, Henry Miller
1997	*The Herbert Huncke Reader*
1998	*The Willow Tree*, Hubert Selby Jr.

Notes

Preface

1. Martin Duberman. *Black Mountain: An Exploration in Community* (New York: E. P. Dutton, 1972), p. 408.

Chapter 1. Forerunners:
The Underground Tradition

1. Kenneth Rexroth, "Disengagement: The Art of the Beat Generation," in *The Beat Generation and the Angry Young Men* (New York: Dell, 1959), p. 351.

2. *Ibid.*

3. Lee Server, *Over My Dead Body: The Sensational Age of the American Paperback (1945–1955)* (San Francisco: Chronicle Books, 1994), pp. 14–15.

4. Dennis McNally, *Desolate Angel: Jack Kerouac, the Beat Generation, and America* (New York: McGraw-Hill, 1979), p. 77.

5. Rexroth, "Disengagement," p. 367.

6. Edmund White, *Genet* (London: Chatto and Windus, 1993), p. 95.

7. *Ibid.*, p. 94.

8. *Ibid.*, p. 174.

9. *Ibid.*, p. 240.

10. Unknown author, review of Kerouac's *On the Road*, in *Survey of Contemporary Literature, vol. 5*, p. 3399.

11. Clement Greenberg, quoted in Irving Sandler, "Avant-Garde Artists of Greenwich Village," in *Greenwich Village Culture and Counterculture* (New Jersey: Rutgers University Press, 1993), p. 320.

12. Martin Green, *New York 1913: The Armory Show and the Paterson Strike Pageant* (New York: Collier Books, 1988), p. 37.

13. Quoted in Daniel Aaron, *Writers on the Left: Episodes in American Literary Communism* (New York: Octagon Books, 1961), p. 228.

14. Leslie Fishbein, "The Culture of Contradiction: The Greenwich Village Rebellion," in Sandler, p. 218.

15. Fred W. McDarrah and Gloria S. McDarrah, *Beat Generation: Glory Days in Greenwich Village* (New York: Schirmer Books, 1996), p. vii.

16. Kingsley Widmer, "The Way Out: Some Literary Sources of the Tough Guy and the Proletarian," in *Tough Guy Writers of the Thirties* (Carbondale: Southern Illinois University Press, 1968), p. 5.

17. *Ibid.*

18. Jay Martin, *Always Merry and Bright* (New York: Penguin, 1980), p. 307.

19. Henry Miller, *Tropic of Cancer* (New York: Grove, 1961), p. 2.

20. *Ibid.*, p. 14.

21. *Ibid.*, p. 10.

22. *Ibid.*, p. 46.

23. Norman Mailer, quoted on the cover of Paul Bowles, *The Delicate Prey and Other Stories* (New York: The Ecco Press).

24. Henry Miller, "Patchen: Man of Anger and Light," in *Stand Still Like the Hummingbird* (New York: New Directions, 1962), p. 32.

25. Christopher Sawyer-Laucanno, *An Invisible Spectator: A Biography of Paul Bowles* (New York: Weidenfeld and Nicholson, 1989).

26. Chester Eisinger, *Fiction of the Forties* (Chicago: University of Chicago Press, 1963), p. 235.

27. John Litweiler, *Ornette Coleman: A Harmolodic Life* (New York: William Morrow, 1992), p. 64.

28. John Clellon Holmes, "The Name of the Game," (*The Beats; Literary Bohemians in Postwar America*, Dictionary of Literary Biography, vol. 16), p. 627.

29. *Ibid.*, 628.

30. Saul Bellow, *Dangling Man* (New York: Avon Books, 1980), p. 126.

31. Lionel Trilling, *Beyond Culture: Essays on Literature and Learning* (New York: Viking, 1965), p. 10.

32. Thomas Hill Schaub, *American Fiction in the Cold War* (Madison: University of Wisconsin Press, 1991), p. 25.

33. Christopher Lasch, *The Agony of the American Left* (New York: Vintage Books, 1969), p. 179.

34. *Ibid.*, p. 181.

35. Rexroth, p. 367.

Chapter 2. The War at Home:
The Novel of Juvenile Delinquency

1. Geoffrey O'Brien, *Hard-Boiled America* (New York: Van Nostrand Reinhold, 1981), p. 131.

2. Willard Motley, *Knock on Any Door* (New York: Appleton Century, 1947), p. 216.

3. Irving Shulman, *The Amboy Dukes* (New York: Pocketbooks, 1971), p. 2.

4. Michael Gordon, *Juvenile Delinquency in the American Novel, 1905–1965* (Bowling Green: Popular Press, 1971), p. 107.

5. Hal Ellson, *Duke* (New York: Popular Library, 1956), p. 59.

6. *Ibid.*, prefatory note.

7. Evan Hunter, *The Blackboard Jungle* (New York: Cardinal, 1955), p. 64.

8. Paul Goodman, *Growing Up Absurd* (New York: Vintage, 1960), p. 152.

9. *Ibid.*, preface, x.

10. *Ibid.*

11. Harlan Ellison, *Web of the City* (New York: Ace, 1983), p. 42.

12. *Ibid.*, p. 6.

13. Leo Margulies, ed., introduction to *The Young Punks* (New York: Pyramid, 1957), n.p.

14. Sol Yurick, *The Warriors* (New York: Pyramid, 1971), p. 37.

15. Quoted in Yurick as epigraph.

16. O'Brien, *Hard-Boiled America*, p. 133.

17. For further information on the phenomenon, see Richard Staehling, "The Truth about Teen Movies," in *Kings of the B's* (New York: E. P. Dutton, 1975), pp. 220–251.

Chapter 3. Hipsters, Beats, and Supermen

1. Holmes, "Name of the Game," p. 627.

2. Jack Kerouac, *The Town and the City* (New York: Harvest Books), p. 362.

3. Chandler Brossard, *Who Walk in Darkness* (New York: Harrow, 1972), p. 107.

4. *Ibid.*, p. 97.

5. *Ibid.*, p. 308.

6. Delmore Schwartz, review of Brossard's novel, in *Partisan Review*, May–June 1952, p. 355.

7. Brossard, *Who Walk in Darkness*, p. 265.

8. Brossard's professional life as an editor for *The New Yorker* and *Time Magazine*, and later as an academic, would seem to further distance him from Beat writing. Still, as his massive, Pynchonesque 1971 novel *Wake Up. We're Almost There* reveals, he was more than willing to explore sexual themes and to experiment with forms that might appeal to the counterculture.

9. John Clellon Holmes, *Go* (New York: Appel, 1977), p. 35.

10. Jack Kerouac, *On the Road*, (New York: Penguin, 1977), p. 97.

11. Michael Davidson, *The San Francisco Renaissance: Poetics and Community at Mid-Century* (New York: Cambridge University Press, 1989), p. 67.

12. Kerouac, *Road*, p. 180.

13. Charles Shuttleworth, "Kerouac's Year at Horace Mann," Kerouac Symposium, The Beat Generation Conference, New York University, May 18, 1994. I am indebted to Charles Shuttleworth, an English teacher at Horace Mann High School, for the following invaluable information on Kerouac's writing for the *Horace Mann Record*. As a student at Horace Mann in 1939 and 1940, Kerouac contributed a series of articles to the school paper on swing bands such as the Count Basie and Glenn Miller Orchestras. Kerouac, at a young age, showed keen insight and a remarkable ability to judge new trends in jazz, especially the importance of Lester Young as a key influence on then current tenor saxophone stylists. Kerouac's mentors who influenced his developing interest in jazz were Seymour Wyse, a British jazz buff with whom Kerouac roomed for a brief time, and Donald Wolf. It is also not generally known that Kerouac acquired knowledge of jazz from George Avakian, the legendary record producer, who was a friend of Kerouac's and a fellow alumnus of Horace Mann. Barry Miles's recent biography of Kerouac also contains information on Kerouac's jazz mentors. See *Jack Kerouac: King of the Beats* (New York: Henry Holt, 1998), pp. 25–26.

14. It is likely that Cassady's influence on Kerouac was nonliterary and that Kerouac was attracted to Cassady's exuberant and uninhibited manner. Neal was a great talker and a charismatic character, and Kerouac's transcriptions of their conversations, recorded in *Visions of Cody* (1972), are probably more revealing of the true nature of Cassady's influence than the letters.

15. Jack Kerouac, *Selected Letters, 1940–1956* (New York: Viking, 1995), p. 226.

16. Norman Mailer, "The White Negro." (San Francisco: City Lights, 1957), n.p.

17. *Ibid.*

18. Mailer, it seems, was attracted not only by Lindner's theories defining the psychopath as an aggressive egotist seeking "instant gratification" but also by Lindner's dramatic writing style. Mailer's prose in "The White Negro" frequently echoes passages by Lindner like this one: "The psychopath is not only a criminal; he is the embryonic Storm-Trooper; he is the disinherited, betrayed antagonist whose aggressions can be mobilized on the instant at which the properly aimed and frustration-evoking formula is communicated by that leader whose tinseled aegis license become law, secret and primitive desires become virtuous ambitions readily attained, and compulsive behavior for-

merly deemed punishable becomes the order of the day." Robert Lindner, *Rebel Without a Cause* (New York: Grove Press), p. 16.

19. Mailer, "White Negro," n.p.

20. Carol Schloss has offered a brilliant and detailed analysis of Mailer's obsession with power throughout his writing career and its relationship to his military experience. See Carol Schloss, *In Visible Light* (New York: Oxford University Press, 1987), pp. 233–249.

21. Norman Mailer, "Hipster and Beatnik: A Footnote to the White Negro," in *Advertisements for Myself* (New York: Berkley-Medallion, 1966), p. 344.

22. *Ibid.*, 346.

23. Norman Mailer, *The Deer Park* (New York: Berkley-Medallion, 1967), p. 282.

24. *Ibid.*

25. Mailer, "Advertisements for Myself on the Way Out," in *Advertisements*, pp. 475–476.

26. Leo Bersani, "The Interpretation of Dreams," in *Norman Mailer: The Man and His Work* (Boston: Little, Brown, 1971), p. 176.

27. Diana Trilling, "The Moral Radicalism of Norman Mailer," in *Man and His Work*, p. 134.

28. C. Wright Mills, *The Power Elite* (New York: Oxford University Press, 1956), p. 7.

29. Ken Kesey, *One Flew Over the Cuckoo's Nest* (New York: Compass, 1964), p. 6.

30. Leslie Fiedler, *The Return of the Vanishing American* (New York: Stein and Day, 1968), p. 185.

Chapter 4. Breaking the Last Taboo: The Gay Novel

1. Gore Vidal, "Sex and the Law," in *The City and the Pillar*, rev. ed. (New York: Signet, 1965), p. 152.

2. The view that homosexuality as subject was relatively common before World War II can be found in James Levin's exhaustive study, *The Gay Novel in America* (New York: Garland, 1991). In addition to the books I have mentioned, Levin explores a myriad of postwar books, most of them written by obscure novelists, and locates homosexual themes. Levin's study is most useful to readers interested in tracking down the subtlest allusions to homosexuality in American fiction of this century.

3. James T. Farrell, "Just Boys," in *The Short Stories of James T. Farrell* (New York: Halcyon House, 1941), p. 98.

4. James Barr, "Random Thoughts on Religion, Homosexuality, and

Playwriting, Not Necessarily to Be Read," introduction to *Game of Fools* (Los Angeles: One Incorporated, 1954), n.p.

5. Vidal, *City and the Pillar*, p. 156.

6. Fritz Peters, *Finestere* (New York: Plume, 1986), p. 119.

7. James Baldwin, *Giovanni's Room* (New York: Signet, 1959), p. 26.

8. Tennessee Williams, "Two on a Party," in *The Short Stories of Tennessee Williams* (New York: Bantam, 1979), p. 307.

9. Graham Caveney, *Gentleman Junkie: The Life and Legacy of William S. Burroughs* (New York: Little, Brown, 1998), p. 161.

10. William S. Burroughs, introduction to *Queer* (New York: Penguin, 1985), vi.

11. *Ibid.*, xxii.

12. A pivotal event in Burroughs's life was his shooting of his wife, Joan, in Mexico. At that moment, Burroughs has claimed, he was brought into contact with "the ugly spirit," which prompted a lifelong struggle against it.

13. Burroughs, *Queer*, p. 63.

14. William S. Burroughs, "Lee's Journals," in *Interzone* (New York: Penguin, 1990), pp. 67–68.

15. *Queer*, p. 124.

16. *Ibid.*, p. 89.

17. Hubert Selby Jr. *Last Exit to Brooklyn* (New York: Black Cat [rev.], 1986), p. 100.

18. John Rechy, *City of Night* (New York: Grove Weidenfeld, 1988), p. 12.

19. John Rechy, *The Sexual Outlaw* (New York: Grove Weidenfeld, 1988), p. 28.

20. David Bergman, *Gaiety Transfigured* (Madison: University of Wisconsin Press, 1991), p. 44.

Chapter 5. Which Way Is Up?: The Drug Novel

1. Drug addiction, like all the taboo subjects I have discussed here, was well represented in cheap, mass-marketed paperback books, circa 1945–1955. The novels, primarily calculated to shock, were, however, rarely faithful to the actual drug milieu, which wasn't accurately presented until Algren, Burroughs, etc.

2. Jean Pierrot, *The Decadent Imagination* (Chicago: University of Chicago Press, 1981), 174–175.

3. John Arthur Maynard, *Venice West* (New York: Rutgers University Press, 1990), p. 95.

4. Bettina Drew, *Nelson Algren: A Life on the Wild Side* (New York: Putnam, 1989), pp. 186–187.

5. Nelson Algren, *The Man with the Golden Arm* (New York: Fawcett), p. 11.

6. George Mandel, *Flee the Angry Strangers* (New York: Bantam, 1953), p. 51.

25. William S. Burroughs, *Junky* (New York: Penguin, 1977), p. xii.

7. By the time Burroughs wrote *Naked Lunch*, he interpreted this police tactic of victimizing drug addicts rather than pushers as an attempt to spread drug use rather than curtail it by forcing pushers to seek new markets. In Burroughs the purpose of invasion is invariably control, particularly when an essential element of the control machine like dope is involved. See Burroughs's interview with Robert Palmer in *Rolling Stone*, May 11, 1972.

8. *Naked Lunch*, p. 197.

9. Quoted in Eric Mottram, *William Burroughs: The Algebra of Need* (London: Calder and Bogus, 1977), p. 30.

10. Maynard, *Venice West*, p. 97.

11. *Ibid.*

12. *Naked Lunch*, p. 164.

13. Mottram, *Algebra of Need*, p. 65.

14. Alfred Chester, "Looking for Genet," in *Commentary* 37, no. 4 (April 1964); p. 67.

15. William S. Burroughs, *Interzone* (New York: Penguin Books, 1990); p. 82.

16. *Interzone*, p. 82.

17. Burroughs, "The Cut-up Method," in *The Moderns* (New York: Corinth Books, 1963), p. 346.

18. Robin Lyndenberg, *Word Cultures: Radical Theory and Practice in William S. Burroughs' Fiction* (Urbana: University of Illinois Press, 1987), p. 75.

19. Ronald Sukenick, *Down and In: Life in the Underground* (New York: Beech Tree Books, 1987), p. 270.

Chapter 6. Capturing the New: The New Journalism

1. Tom Wolfe interview in *The New Fiction: Interviews with Innovative American Writers* (Chicago: University of Illinois Press, 1971), p. 77.

2. *Ibid.*, p. 83.

3. Tom Wolfe, ed., *The New Journalism* (New York: Harper and Row, 1973), p. 32.

4. Wolfe interview, *New Fiction*, p. 83.

5. *Ibid.*, p. 94.

6. Wolfe, *New Journalism*, p. 45.

7. Morris Dickstein, *Gates of Eden: American Culture in the Sixties* (New York: Basic Books, 1977), p. 137.

8. Hunter S. Thompson, *Hell's Angels: Fear and Loathing in California* (New York: Ballantine Books, 1975), p. 46.

9. Howard Kohn, "Hell's Angels: Masters of Menace," *Rolling Stone,* April 5, 1979, p. 59.

10. Thompson, p. 271.

11. Kohn, pp. 56–64.

12. Tom Wolfe interview, *Rolling Stone,* August 21, 1980, p. 36.

13. Tom Wolfe, *The Electric Kool-Aid Acid Test* (New York: Farrar, Strauss, and Giroux, 1968), p. 395.

14. Ed Sanders, introduction to *The Family* (New York: Avon, 1972), p. 14.

15. Renato Poggioli, in *The Theory of the Avant-Garde* (New York: Harper and Row, 1971); David Daiches, "Politics and Literary Imagination," in *Liberations: New Essays on the Humanities in Revolution,* ed. Ihab Hassan (Middletown: Wesleyan University Press, 1971). Both identify politically reactionary elements within bohemian protest.

16. Mailer, "White Negro."

17. Sanders, *Family*, p. 23.

18. Sanders speculates that the motive for the Tate murders may have been Manson's artistic rejection by Terry Melcher, a frequent guest at the home of Polanski. But, as Stoddard Martin suggests, behind the whole killing spree "lurks a force too often overlooked: the angry resentment of the native hipster for jet-set beautiful people." Stoddard Martin, *Art, Messianism, and Crime* (New York: St. Martin's, 1986), p. 184.

19. Norman Mailer, *The Armies of the Night* (New York: New American Library, 1968), p. 65.

20. Jack Richardson. "The Aesthetics of Norman Mailer," in *Norman Mailer: The Man and His Work*, p. 197.

21. Mailer, *Armies*, p. 66.

Chapter 7. The Age of Monsters: Dominance and Submission in the 1960s

1. In addition to publishing books by Samuel Beckett, D. H. Lawrence, and the Marquis de Sade, Barney Rossett, a legendary figure in the book trade who had purchased the company in 1952, fought numerous legal battles challenging obscenity laws, winning the right to publish *Tropic of Cancer, Naked Lunch,* and *Last Exit to Brooklyn.* With the rise of the counterculture in the 1960s, Rossett was quick to reprint or collect for the first time the work of underground authors who had had little exposure in the 1950s. Alexander Trocchi and Michael Rumaker were two such authors.

2. Quoted in Richard Seaver, Introduction to *Cain's Book*, by Alexander Trocchi (New York: Grove 1997), xi.

3. Many of Olympia's books, including *Lolita*, *Watt*, and *Naked Lunch*, were eventually published in the United States by Grove Press. Rossett shared Girodias's sharp editorial eye for challenging and controversial writing.

4. Seaver, introduction, xiii.

5. *Ibid.*

6. Alexander Trocchi, *Young Adam*, in *The Outsiders* (New York: Signet Books, 1961), p. 66.

7. *Ibid.*, p. 108.

8. Randall Stevenson, *The British Novel Since the Thirties* (Athens: University of Georgia Press), p. 129.

9. Michael Rumaker, "Gringos," in *Gringos and Other Stories* (New York: Grove Press, 1968), pp. 47–48.

10. Michael Rumaker, "The Use of the Unconscious in Writing," in *New American Story* (New York: Grove Press, 1965), p. 275.

11. Robert Stone, *A Hall of Mirrors* (Boston: Houghton Mifflin, 1964), pp. 5–6.

12. Robert Solotaroff, *Robert Stone*, (New York: Twayne, 1994), p. 28.

13. Quoted in Solotaroff, *Robert Stone*, p. 27.

14. John Tytell, *Naked Angels: The Lives and Literature of the Beat Generation* (New York: McGraw-Hill Paperback Edition, 1977), p. 208.

15. Jack Kerouac, *Big Sur* (New York: Bantam Books, 1963), p. 36.

16. Ann Charters, *Kerouac* (San Francisco: Straight Arrow Books, 1973), p. 323.

17. Kerouac, *Big Sur*, 167.

18. Quoted in McNally, *Desolate Angel*, p. 242.

19. John W. Crowley, *The White Logic: Alcoholism and Gender in American Modernist Fiction* (Amherst: University of Massachusetts Press, 1994), p. 140.

20. Kerouac, *Big Sur*, pp. 89–90.

21. Charters, *Kerouac*, p. 334.

22. Kerouac, *Big Sur*, p. 174.

Conclusion

1. Kerouac addressed the threat of confrontation in his essay "The Vanishing Hobo," and, as has been shown, in the tragic novel *Big Sur* the stage was set for his own self-destruction.

2. Since the 1970s gay novelists have depicted homosexuals as socially well adjusted, possibly perceiving that the political struggle would best be served

by a more conservative approach than that which was presented in the sixties by Rechy and other underground writers.

3. Robert Draper, *Rolling Stone Magazine: The Uncensored History* (New York: Harper Perennial, 1991), p. 225.

4. Martin, *Art*, pp. 56–57.

5. Gregory Stephenson, *The Daybreak Boys: Essays on the Literature of the Beat Generation* (Carbondale: Southern Illinois University Press, 1990), p. 15.

6. Seymour Krim, quoted in James Dickey's foreword to *The Complete Short Stories of Thomas Wolfe* (New York: Charles Scribner's Sons, 1987), xi.

7. Rechy, *Sexual Outlaw*, p. 300.

Index

Index